INVESTING MADE SIMPLE AND EASY

THE 49 ESSENTIAL PERSONAL FINANCE, WEALTH MANAGEMENT, AND TRADING TIPS THAT PROS SHOULD SHARE

NORMANDEAU, FRANCK

CONTENTS

INTRODUCTION

I've been working in finance for over 20 years now, and I have noticed, to my great consternation, that the vast majority of people still don't understand "the Game" or, at the very least, how the game is played.

I consider myself a finance freak; I eat finance for breakfast, lunch, dinner, and as a snack at night before bedtime. I even sometimes secretly get up during the night to eat some more. In the past, I've been fortunate enough to come across a multitude of articles and books that have inspired me to the highest degree and made me a better investor. Books such as "The little book of Behavioral Investment" by James Montier, "Open letter to irresponsible investors" by André Gosselin, "The Wealthy Barber" by David Chilton, "The Slight Edge" by Jeff Olson or "Security Analysis" by Graham & Dodd. These books are, in my opinion, a "must" for anyone serious about mastering the art of investing.

If you're not the type of person who is passionate about finance and reading the three lines of economic news that your smartphone force-feeds you every morning is enough to make you feel nauseous until lunchtime, then this book is for you. I understand that you probably have better things to do than read 5000 pages of financial theory and that even if you do have the time, indigestion will hit you long before the end of the 100th page. That's precisely why I wrote this book. What I'm offering you here is just the candy and none of the veggies. I offer you the punch of the movie before the end, the final score before the game. I offer you a condensed, summarized, and re-condensed version of the best books, articles, and financial concepts I've read in the last 20 years, to which I add my own twist, of course. Liquid food for your brain that will go in by itself and won't be hard to digest.

My commitment to you...

I won't make you finance experts; I won't give you my very best formulas that only an expert could understand. I will not lose you with concepts and terminology of intellectuals and, I hope, will not make you nauseous.

What I want to do...

To educate you in a simple, fast, and pleasant way, to make you better investors, and ultimately to allow you to get rich... Why not?

If that's your cup of tea, then turn the page, and let's jump right into it...

OUR PREDISPOSITION TO FAILURE / LET'S KILL JOE

What do you mean, Franck? We are predisposed to failure? What I mean is that our brains are basically designed to make us all bad investors. Our brain play tricks on us and don't necessarily have the same priorities as your accountant. Indeed, imagine that your brain is composed of two little guys who have two completely different personalities.

First of all, there is JOE. Joe is a man of action. He's quick like a cat, courageous and robust while remaining close to his emotions.

Then there is SHERLOCK. SHERLOCK is more of an intellectual, logical, deductive, and analytical type. SHERLOCK likes to take his time.

OK, I'll stop you right now if you compare yourself to JOE or SHERLOCK. Don't waste your time. We are all both JOE and

SHERLOCK. It is true that some people are indeed more JOE than SHERLOCK and vice versa, but in general, we are both. Remember the last time you watched a horror movie or one of those jump scare clips you find on Youtube. You know it's only a movie, you know you are in no way in danger, but none the less when the scary guy with the chainsaw pops unexpectedly out of the dark corner, you jump in your seat, hide your face, step back or just reach for the remote to press mute because it's less scary that way. Well, you've just met JOE. A few seconds later, you tell yourself: "I'm so silly; I knew this was just a silly movie and therefore was in no real danger." Congratulations, you have just met SHERLOCK. Want another example? Notice the next time you bump your toes on a chair leg. Your first instinct will probably be to swear at the chair, maybe even take a wack at it. As an inanimate object, the chair probably does not deserve this treatment. Again, JOE spoke first. In fact, SHERLOCK is most likely laughing at JOE right now.

Don't think that makes you less of a person. It just makes you a normal person. You see, JOE is made to speak first; it's all about survival. When something attacks you, who cares if it's a scary guy with a chainsaw, a snake, or a mean chair, it's way better to get out of there first and then figure out if it was necessary than to stand there and take two minutes to figure out if it is indispensable to get out. It's like having the information go to JOE and SHERLOCK simultaneously, but taking the Autobahn 12-lane wide superhighway in the first case and the scenic country road in the second. There is a way to measure whether you are more JOE or more SHERLOCK. In fact, a Yale professor, Shane Frederick*, has created a short test of three easy questions designed to determine how much JOE and SHERLOCK you are. Take the test with me for fun...

1. A baseball bat and a ball cost $1.10. Knowing that the bat costs $1.00 more than the ball, how much does the ball cost?
2. If it takes 5 minutes for five machines to create five widgets, how long would it take 100 machines to create 100 widgets?
3. A lake is partially covered by a patch of lily pads. Every day, the patch portion of the lake double in size. If it takes 48 days for the patch to cover the entire lake, how many days does it take to cover half of the lake?

Each of these questions has an obvious answer, so if you let JOE answer each of these questions, your answers will probably be 10 cents for the baseball, 100 minutes for the 100 widgets, and 24 days to cover the lake. All three of these answers may be very obvious but are entirely wrong. However, if SHERLOCK answered these questions, your answers would be more like $0.05 for the baseball (if the ball was worth $0.10, the bat would cost $1.10, and the total would be $1.20). 5 minutes to make the 100 widgets (each machine produces 1 widget every 5 minutes) and 47 days to cover half the lake (if the patch doubles every day and at days 48, the lake is completely covered, well, the day before it was half-covered). Don't go jumping off the bridge if you got it wrong here; Shane Frederick gave the test to 3500 academics, and only 17% got it all right, while twice more (33%) got it all wrong. All you can conclude from your result is that if you got it all wrong, you need to be careful about an emotional response. In contrast, you should be cautious about overconfidence if you got it all right.

I remember it like it was yesterday; it's November 2016, a few days before the American election, and a crazy rumor started to circulate: **Donald Trump could be elected**. I couldn't believe my ears, but this would not be our first election scandal, so caution was required. I decided to contact all my clients to inform them of my intention to temporarily sell all our equity positions. At least for the election period. Our performance since the beginning of the year doubled the benchmarks, so the way I saw it, we could afford to lose a week's return, and in my opinion, if by I don't know what miracle Mr. Trump was to be elected, although very unlikely, the markets would suffer in the most brutal way. Surprise, surprise, it's election night, and it's now official: Donald Trump is the new American president. My first reflex is to look at the future indices on the different world markets, which gives me a taste of the day that awaits me tomorrow. To no big surprise, the markets are down by -9%, and the news is still very fresh. It will be a long night for people who didn't bother to do what I did the night before. I'm going to bed with a sense of accomplishment and sleeping like a baby because none of this affects my clientele. I know what to expect tomorrow. I will receive call after call from clients who will throw me flowers for my vision and skill. In short, life is good. The next morning, the first thing I do when I open my eyes I grab my cell phone to see where the markets are now. Down 12%, down 14%, maybe even down 16%? Who knows... But to my surprise, we are only at -2%. Now I'm wondering what exactly happened during the night to explain this turnaround? Was this all just a dream or a bad joke, maybe? No, Donald Trump is indeed the new president, and on top of it, he has a majority. Still puzzled, I listen to Bloomberg in the car on the way to the office but get no answer. It's now 11:00am, and Hilary Clinton is about to make her speech to the nation; and not surprisingly, she's pulling out the classic speech that almost every loser for 200 years uses. You know the kind: "I am obviously disappointed with the result but will none the less congratulate and line up behind our new president and ask all my supporters to do the same for a strong and united country blablabla....". It was at that very moment that it all clicked in my head. In other words, that's when Sherlock finally joined the party. Sherlock knew how to put emotion aside and understood that, for the time being, at least, the current scenario was nothing less than the best possible outcome. Sherlock understood that having a majority government would provide a much better environment for the stock markets. Sherlock also understood that Super Donald, with some of his campaign promises, especially his tax cuts, would positively impact the markets (at least in the short term). Sherlock even understood that the markets like stability and that having Hilary on the losing side would bring more stability than Trump (who was screaming foul before he even lost the election). It was, therefore, at this precise moment that I decided to reinstate my initial positions. At that point, the markets had recovered almost all of their losses. In the end, all of this may not save as much, if not a drop of -0.2%, but at least allowed me and several clients to sleep like babies.

. . .

WHAT YOU NEED TO REMEMBER HERE IS THAT YOUR FIRST response is always your emotional response and usually the worst when it comes to talking about investing. In an ideal world, SHERLOCK would kill JOE. We'd be in business to invest (although in much worse shape the next time we find ourselves in front of a mad man with a chainsaw).

With that being said, there is light at the end of the tunnel. Now that we are aware of our vulnerability, we have a significant advantage over all the JOEs "Out There."

To use an old saying: "A fool who is a fool but knows he is a fool is a lot less foolish than a fool who is a fool but doesn't know he is a fool."

YOU ARE YOUR OWN WORST ENEMY / 9 TRAPS YOU WILL MOST LIKELY PUT ON YOUR PATH

Franck, are you telling me that if it wasn't enough to have a predisposition to failure, we will have to fight against ourselves to achieve our goals?

Well... Yes!

As Warren Buffett once said, "Investing is simple but not easy. You want to become a master in the art of investing; well, I'm sorry to tell you, but there are still a series of vulnerabilities and pitfalls that you will have to avoid.

FIRST TRAP: ALWAYS TRYING TO BE RIGHT. (NARCISSISM)

Play a game with me. I give you three numbers (5, 10, 15) and ask you to find the rule I used to build the sequence. You can propose as many new series as you want, and for each of your series, I will tell you if the rule applies or not. If you are like most people, your first sequence will look like (10, 15, 20) or (20, 25, 30). And if I tell you that these series do indeed fit my rule, you'll know for sure that my rule is something like a series of numbers that goes up by five. Which is all wrong. The reality is that your sequences have not taught you anything new. In fact, you didn't even try to learn anything. Your sequences were simply meant to confirm a preconceived idea you had about my rule. Your goal was never to discover new information that would ultimately help you find the solution. It was to confirm that you were right.

You see, it is in failure that we really learn something. Many discoveries that changed the world were the result of mistakes: Penicillin (Alexander Fleming), radiation (Marie Curie), gravity (Isaac Newton), plastic (Charles Goodyear), the Pacemaker (Wilson Greatbatch), even Corn Flakes (John Kellogg). OK, I admit that maybe Corn Flakes didn't change the world, but you get the concept nonetheless.

Thomas J. Watson, the founder of IBM, had a saying: "The formula for success is quite simple: Double your rate of failure."

To get back to our little game, it's only by being wrong that you could have ended up being right. Ironic, isn't it? Indeed, if you had told me (10, 3, 1) or (15, 10, 5) and I had answered you a big fat NO. Then and only then would you have really learned something concrete. My rule was ascending numbers, so (2, 5, 100 156 000 851) would have been a good sequence too. But the only way to figure it out for sure, not guess it, was to ultimately make me tell you no.

You are probably wondering where I am going with this. Well, as human beings, we like being right much more than being wrong. We are constantly trying, consciously or unconsciously, to be correct and to confirm our preconceived ideas. So if you have a preconceived idea about something that interests you and start researching it, your brain will instinctively pull out anything that confirms what you already think while ignoring the rest.

I do the same thing all the time. I'm shopping for a hotel I look at the comments of travelers who have stayed at the same hotel in the past and read only the positive comments and discredit the negative ones: "That's an old comment", "People's expectations are too high", etc... I do the same thing when I read reviews of a movie I really want to see: "They're not real fans", "It's not a big deal, I haven't read the book", "It's just young people who have made comments", etc.

One of the most extreme examples of this is the story of Sir Roger Tichborne. The only son of a wealthy English Baroness was presumed dead in a shipwreck in 1854. Surprise, surprise, the prodigy child returns home after an absence of 12 years to claim his place as the family's rightful heir. The only problem

is that the so-called son is a few inches taller and has a much much larger build than his so-called alter-ego. OK, you'll tell me that it's possible to grow up and gain weight. However, it was a little more complicated in 1860 to make tattoos disappear, change the color of one's eyes, stop speaking your mother tongue, and have birthmarks disappear. Although all the signs indicated without a doubt that this man was an impostor, the Baroness found a way to ignore all the evidence. It was only after the Baroness's death that the family was able to prove the true identity of Arthur Orton, the butcher from the nearby village, which earned the impostor a stay in prison for the next 10 years. The Baroness was so desperate to find her lost son that she simply ignored all the contradictory signs.

This kind of behavior can cost a lot of money in investment, but fortunately, there is a trick to it. Charles Darwin used to analyze only the opinions contradictory to his own, and I would say that it served him well. When making an investment decision (like any other decision for that matter), make a list of the PROS and CONS **but without the PROS.**

Bruce Berkowitz of Fairholme Capital Management pushes this concept to the extreme. When considering an investment, he tries to kill the company rather than trying to find information that would support the investment. He considers every possible scenario, whether it's a recession, inflation, earthquake, zooming interest rate, or a bomb going off. If he can't kill it, maybe he's onto something.

In other words, for a moment, become the most pessimistic version of yourself, starting with the premise that everything is never all black or all white. Find all the black and make a list. Not the white stuff. Your head is already filled with it; we don't want more. Then go through your list and determine if you can live with all that black. If you can, that decision may well be the right one. What's more, this exercise will also allow you to be aware of the vulnerability of your investment, which will later allow you to react appropriately if the situation requires it.

I'm the kind of optimistic guy who usually sees the glass as half full. But when it comes to analyzing an investment, it's much better to see the glass as half empty. See it completely empty if you want; that's even better.

~

CASE STUDY PART 1

Several years ago, in the middle of a Thanksgiving family dinner, while I was still working on my second piece of sugar pie, my brother-in-law approached me to tell me about this tip from a friend at work concerning this unknown pharmaceutical company *"Slim."* He went on and on talking about *"Slim"* and their revolutionary product in the field of weight loss destined for a bright future. Initially slightly insulted, I went into a skeptical mode before becoming intrigued. The next day, I went online to research

Slim only to realize that the company in question is not only real; they are indeed doing research in the weight loss field and are indeed about to get their endorsement from the FDA (Food and Drug Association) for the marketing of a new product. I watch many videos that report the miracle results of the product in question and even go so far as to read several analyzes from an impressive number of doctors who confirm that this is very real. My research, therefore, with the feeling of accomplishment because after all I have done my homework, I decide to go ahead and invest in the company in question. But did I actually do my homework?

> *NO, my research was intended to confirm what I wanted to confirm, not to uncover new information that would ultimately allow me to rationally determine whether the investment was appropriate or not. In no way did my research reveal that Slim was crippled by debt, facing numerous lawsuits and that their CEO was on his fifth company in four years (the previous four having failed miserably.)*

SECOND TRAP: TOO MUCH IS LIKE NOT ENOUGH. (OVERCOMPLICATING)

Sometimes with all the best intentions, we tend to overdo it. We go out there and find out everything there is to know about the investment we are considering. In the end, most of the time, we end up paralyzing ourselves by overwhelming information and we end up doing nothing. In police work, they call it an orgy of evidence. Too much is like not enough. Instead of collecting all possible information, and trust me, there is plenty you should focus your energy on getting the important information to you.

Not too long ago, my son was looking at buying an electric bike. That's a significant expense for him; in fact, most of the money he earned this summer, working 6 days per week at 3 different jobs, will go toward this purchase, so I don't need to tell you that he wants to do this right. He then started the research process. Two weeks later, my son collected an impressive amount of data about almost all e-bikes available out there. All sorts of data like types of frame, class, hub-drive motor, mid-drive motor, wattage, charging time, number of batteries, battery types, integrated battery, external battery, torque, pedal assist level, smartphone integration, security system, suspension, fork, crankset, shifters, derailleur, gears, brakes, rims, tires and so many more. A few weeks later, I asked my son if he had finally chosen a bike, and to my surprise, he told me that he was further away from finding his bike than he was when he started the whole thing. TOO MUCH IS LIKE NOT ENOUGH. Then I asked my son:

> ***- OK, forget about all this crap. Why did you
>   really want an electric bike in the first place?***
> *-To go see my friends, even the one who lives
>   further, without spending too much energy in
>   the process.*
> ***-OK, so what you need is something with a good
>   range. What else?***
> *-I'd like it to be fast?*
> ***-Obviously. Anything else?***
> *-Well, it would be nice if it had big tires to go off-
>   road as well and look cool.*
> ***-That's it?***
> *-That's it.*

So at the end of the day, the only thing my son needed to look at was four things, range, max speed, tires, and of course, overall appearance. Funny enough, most of these properties were not even part of his whole data collection. My son purchased the perfect e-bike within the hour following our conversation.

The same thing goes for any investment. The amount of information available is way too large for you to even consider gathering it all. Even if you manage to do so, paralysis will hit you like a ton of bricks way before you manage to analyze it all. Trust me, I tried. Just focus on meaningful information that make sense to you, I have a system based on 50 different points of information (28 quantitative, 22 qualitative). It may seem like a lot, but it's, in fact, 50 out of many thousands.

A recent study* was done to prove that less is more when it comes to decision making. Participants were asked to select the best of four different cars in the study. One of the cars was clearly a better choice, 75% of its attributes being better than the other three cars. At first, they gave the group only 4 attributes per car and asked them to choose; 60% of the participants picked the best car. The second time they gave the group 12 attributes per car (including the original 4) and asked them to choose the best car. This time, only 20% ended up picking the right car. Additionally, when asked about the level of confidence in their car selection, the candidates seem to be way more confident in their analysis with the 12 attributes than were they only had 4.

CASE STUDY PART 2

Although I already made the investment, a little voice in the back of my head (Sherlock) is telling me that maybe I haven't been as thorough in my analysis of "Slim" as I should have been and that maybe I should go back to it. After all, since I just made the purchase 2 days ago and nothing has moved so far, it's still not too late to get out of it if something comes up.

But this time, I will do things right. I will leave no stone unturned and collect every little bit of information about this company. My research generates hundreds and hundreds of pages of reviews, analyses, financial statements, ratios, medical research papers, articles and blogs. Many days went by, and I managed to go through not even 2% of all the stuff I collected. I now realize that this will take me years and that by the time I'm done, new data will become available, and all the information I collected will be outdated. It's an impossible task. Anyways, it's been 2 weeks since my purchase of "Slim," and it's already up 5%, so that little voice in my head shuts up, and I'm now confident I made the right move. These whole 2 weeks may seem like a big waste of time, but at the end of the day, I'm better than I was 2 weeks ago, right?

> *NO, you are not better off, and YES, those 2 weeks have been a complete waste of time. Your research took your focus away from what you should have concentrated on. I'm sorry to tell you, but you are more blind than ever.*

THIRD TRAP: SOMETIMES IT'S OVER EVEN IF IT'S NOT. (STUBBORNNESS)

<u>**CASE#1***</u>: You are the president of a pharmaceutical company and have spent 90 million dollars researching a new revolutionary drug that will cure baldness. While you have completed 90% of the project, a competitor firm comes out with its own drug to cure baldness. To make the letters worse, their drug is in every way, far better and more economical than yours will ever hope to be. What do you do? Do you spend the 10 million dollars needed to complete yours?

Interestingly enough, 80% of people will tell you to spend the $10 million needed to complete the drug.

· · ·

CASE#2: YOU ARE THE PRESIDENT OF A PHARMACEUTICAL company and receive a recommendation from one of your researchers to spend $1,000,000 on a drug that will cure baldness. Your top competitor already has its own drug to cure baldness. Their drug is far better and more economical than yours will ever hope to be. What is your decision?

Curiously, 80% of people will tell you not to spend the $1,000,000 needed to complete.

I don't know if it's because it takes us a lot of time and effort to get the machine going that we're willing to continue in the wrong direction even though we're aware of our eventual failure, but it seems that after a certain point, we're not able to let go. In poker, we call this "Pot Committed."

I hope you realize that ironically, most people are willing to spend $10 million on a losing cause just because one is committed when they consider it too expensive 10 times less money to get the same thing if no $ $$$ has been spent to date.

The same thing happens all the time in investing. You will face surprises; it's inevitable. You'll have to constantly ask yourself, "Is this new information a game-changer? Forget what you've done in the past. Today, in light of all the available information, would you do the same thing if you had to do it again? If the answer is yes, then you stay the course. If not, you may want to reconsider your strategy.

CASE STUDY (PART 3)

Five frustrating months have now passed since the day I decided to invest 20% of my portfolio in Slim. Now at -50%, I still hold my position in the company and wonder if I should still stay the course. The famous approval of the FDA (Food and Drug Association) for the launch of the new product is still pending. At the same time, some competitors of Slim have already successfully marketed products strangely similar to that of Slim. That said, I know that in investing, you have to buy low and sell high, so I decided to double my position. Good or bad strategy?

> *Bad. Go back in time. Based on all the information you have today and assuming you never invested in Slim in the first place. Would you make this investment today? Surely not. Doubling its position can be a good strategy if the fundamental of the investment remains interesting, which is not the case here (Pot Committed).*

FOURTH TRAP: WHEN THE STORY TAKES OVER. (PERSUASION)

Today is your lucky day because I will allow you to benefit from a fantastic deal. You see, for a limited time, you will have access to this exceptional opportunity which will make all your loved ones jealous. Indeed, for a limited time, I will share with you the best-kept secret in the world, the trick that all Hollywood stars have understood, blablablablablablablabla… Your success depends only on you, pick up the phone and change your life! But that's not all! If you proceed in the next 15 minutes, I will not only reduce to only 3 payments of $69.99 instead of 4, but I will also give you my exercise book and two/three useless gadgets that are worth less than their packaging. A brand value of $399.99 all that for the modest sum of blablabla..... Add a few testimonials from good-looking actors, highly paid to swear that this product has changed their lives, and you have the whole nine yard.

We get all too often sucked into a lovely story filled with beautiful promises. It's probably the oldest sales technique in the world, but it's still one of the most effective... you've all seen one of these infomercials whose goal is to convince you to buy some "Made in China" widget that will solve a problem you didn't have before...

If you are one of those who think that this kind of thing doesn't work, think again! Not only does it work, but it works very well. Talk about Mr. Shamwow, who became a multimillionaire by making big WOW on TV. Or "Snuggie," which has made over 400 million dollars.

What you need to understand is that a considerable part responsible for the success of this kind of selling method is related to the sense of urgency. Why? Because whoever is selling you whatever, they want Joe to take the decision, not Sherlock. If that infomercial URO CLUB (PS: check it out, you'll have a good laugh) was telling you this offer will be available for the next 30 days, they wouldn't have sold half as many as they did (they probably would not sell any). In fact, it reminds me of a tip I read many years ago to help people reduce impulsive purchases. A woman wrote to her advisor to ask for help. That woman was a compulsive buyer, and she would end up buying every infomercial product she would watch. The advisor's tip was to use a large Tupperware container, fill it with water, insert her credit card in the middle, and put it in the freezer. Then the next time, she felt the urge to purchase one of those infomercial products, go to the freezer, take out the container, flip it in the sink and wait for the card to unfreeze. If she still felt the need to make the purchase by the time the card was accessible, she should go ahead. If not, put the card back in the water and the container back in the freezer until next time. That simple trick gave plenty of time for Sherlock to speak up, and the client in question ended up cutting 80% of her credit card expense.

You may think right now that this doesn't concern you because you never bought a product from an infomercial. You still need to realize that this kind of rose water sales technique, where you are promised the so-called "DEAL" of the century, where you are enticed by the prowess of unbelievable PAST RESULTS and try to create in you a SENSE OF URGENCY, is not exclusive to infomercials. These are often the same techniques used by your corner convenience store, grocery store, and, yes, even your investment advisor: "Hello, Mr. Bolduc. I have an excellent opportunity for you (DEAL). Not only is this investment super cheap, but it has made an average return of 20% per year over the last five years, (PAST RESULTS). My inventory is almost depleted, but I kept some for you if you wish to act on this today (SENSE OF URGENCY).

The best example in investing is, without a doubt, new share issues (IPOs). It's always the same story: the company in question is praised as being extraordinary, having generated a small fortune in the past, with a bright future and a strong position in its industry. In short, an absolute gold mine that is offered to you at a meager price for a limited time. Sounds familiar? Infomercials.

I don't know about you, but if I were the owner of this fantastic company and the future looked as good as they say it does, well, the last thing I'd want to do is share the spoils with a bunch of shareholders. On the other hand, if the future isn't so rosy and I can see hard times ahead, I'd love to have lots of friends to split the bill with me. Not convinced? What if I told you that in the United States* from 1980 to 2007, IPOs underperformed the markets by 21% annually during the first three years following their launch? In Canada, from 2000 to 2012, IPOs underperformed by an average of 16% in the first year and are still underperforming even after 5 years...

Friendly advice: When it's too good to be true... It probably is. Don't be fooled by the good stories and give time to Sherlock to have a say.

CASE STUDY (PART 4)

Another -25% later, I've had enough. I call the brother-in-law to thank him, ironically of course, for the tip and inform him of my intention to take my losses and move on to another call. He tells me to wait because his source has informed him that the company is about to do a new IPO on the American market soon, which will attract a lot of new capital and give a lot of visibility to the company. So I decided to give the runner one last chance and wait for the IPO. Because, I have nothing left to lose anyways and because it's true that, technically, I haven't lost until I've sold. True?

> *False. With the initial investment of 20% and the addition of 10%, even with the losses assumed, Slim still represents a position of 15% of the portfolio, which does not qualify as "nothing to lose." As for not losing until you sell, go tell that to the thousand of investors who still have their Nortel stocks in their portfolio and watch their reactions for fun.*

FIFTH TRAP: LOSING FOCUS. (DISTRACTION)

Often, being too close to a situation prevents us from seeing it as a whole. I've always liked the experiment of D.J Simon and C.F Chabris, two American researchers who focused on what they call involuntary blindness. In an experiment, they asked participants to watch a basketball game between two teams (black shirts vs. white shirts) and count the number of passes completed between the white players. In the middle of the clip, a man dressed in a gorilla suit takes place in the middle of the court, beats his chest (a la King Kong), and quietly walks off the court. At the end of the clip, the participants are asked how many passes have taken place. The majority of the candidates have the correct answer. They are then asked if they have seen the gorilla, and 60% of the candidates have simply not seen it. We have the candidates watch the film again. All the candidates that did not see the gorilla in the first place say that the film has been changed and that the gorilla did not appear in the original video. The gorilla is so obvious now; how could that be otherwise. The experiment shows that because the candidates are focused on counting passes, they lose sight of the big picture.

The same thing constantly happens in investing. We become so obsessed with specific details that we lose focus. It's inevitable; every time we look back on a stock market crash, we conclude that the signs were more than obvious. We simply, at some point, stopped looking. We were too busy making money.

Sometimes it is necessary to stop and take a step back to regain the big picture.

~

CASE STUDY (PART 5)

Slim continues to plummet into what seems like an endless pit as the IPO is slow and slow to come. Slim is becoming a real obsession for me. I check my cell phone 12 times a day to see if there is any development in the IPO file. I am in constant communication with the brother-in-law, who is starting to regret giving me the tip in the first place. Slim's IPO is all that matters at this point; everything else is just a distraction. True?

> *False. Looking too closely sometimes leads to losing the overview. The new IPO constitutes a dilution of the company's value, which will not improve the situation. In fact, it will most likely even make it worse.*

SIXTH TRAP: I AM EITHER GOOD OR UNLUCKY. (ARROGANCE)

Our self-esteem makes us have a bad habit of attributing our good moves (internal factor) and looking for excuses for our bad moves (external factor). The best example of this is probably in sports. Notice the next time you watch a hockey game (or any other sport for that matter). Listen to the post-game comments. The players on the winning team will probably tell you how well prepared they were, how they followed the game plan to the letter, how opportunistic they were, how the special units made a difference, or how Carey stole another one for the team (internal factors)... **Translation: we're good**.

Now listen to the comments of the players of the losing team: We played well, but we were unlucky, we hit 3 posts, the referee made some questionable calls, the puck wasn't rolling for us tonight, we were up against a goalie in great shape, we had to deal with injuries, it was the second game in two nights (external factors)... **Translation: it's not our fault.**

NEWS FLASH: SOMETIMES, WE JUST DON'T HAVE IT. It is essential to learn from our mistakes, but we must acknowledge our mistakes to do so. Our inability to blame ourselves for our failures means that we tend to repeat them instead of evolving. I'm willing to bet a shiny toonie that the team that loses the hockey game and apologizes for it by saying that they were just unlucky will probably lose the next game against that same opponent as well. But if that team recognizes that they were outmatched and concludes that their failure was due to the fact that playing physical against a fast team with such a devastating power play was the wrong strategy. That the line choices were inappropriate and that when you play against a talented goalie, you have to get traffic in front of the net if you hope to score. Their chance of improving next time will be much better.

In investment, it's the same thing. You have to be modest <u>in the good and bad times </u>and learn from your mistakes; and mistakes you will make, guaranteed. Lack of modesty hurts when making the wrong moves but be careful because it hurts even more when making the good moves. Let's be honest; sometimes, you make a good move for the wrong reasons. Refusing to acknowledge it when it happens is even more damaging because you won't always be lucky. You might be tempted to cross the highway on foot to avoid a detour, and you might even survive it. That doesn't mean it was a good idea or that you should do it again.

The outcome Matrix

	POSITIVE RESULT	**NEGATIVE RESULT**
GOOD REASONING	Deserved success	Bad Luck
BAD REASONING	Dumb Luck	Poetic justice

I am a big fan of poker, not for the money but for the strategic side of the game. To manipulate your opponents psychologically, make statistics (without looking like a geek), and have the right to lie (bluff) as you please. How can you not like this game? I ask you. But in the end, poker is still a game of probability. I have introduced many of my friends and family members to poker. When you play poker with a new player, it's only a matter of time before that player doesn't play rationally, goes against all odds, but gets saved by the gods of luck and wins the hand. It is at this very moment that I just took a serious option on winning the whole game. You see, people often tend to associate the quality of their actions with the results obtained. I won the hand, so I did well. No matter that the odds were 1,000,000 to 1, I won the hand, so it was the right thing to do. As your poker opponent, I want you to think so because now that the one hand out of 1,000,000 that could save you has passed, I will now collect on the next 999,999. Winning that hand was probably the worst thing that could have happened to you because you are now convinced that your actions were appropriate when they were not. It's true that some people seem to be born under a lucky star, but personally, I would avoid overdoing it. Luck always runs out in the end.

In short, although it is relatively easy to attribute your good moves to yourself, it is essential to recognize when you have been off track, regardless of the outcome. After all, maybe Lady Luck saved the day this time.

∼

CASE STUDY (PART 6)

Slim's IPO is finally approved, but the timing couldn't be worse as the markets are starting to run out of steam and the average investor only has eyes for big companies offering big dividends. The current climate, combined with the anticipation of a possible recession, does not offer the expected visibility for Slim, which explains the disappointing results of the long-awaited IPO. In the end, it seems that bad luck hangs over me.

NO, maybe Slim's IPO failed because investors
realized what I still refuse to admit: Slim just

> *isn't a good investment. Luck has nothing to*
> *do here.*

SEVENTH TRAP: BELIEVING TOO HIGHLY OF YOURSELF. (OVERCONFIDENCE)

You put 100 people together in a room ask them if they believe that they are taller, more intelligent, faster, a better cook, or a better lover than the average of the group, and I can guarantee you that for each of those questions, 70-80% of people will say yes. It makes me think of a celeb quote from Yogi Berra: "Baseball is 90% mental and the other half physical". I'm sorry, Yogi, but it doesn't add up.

Overconfidence and arrogance may seem like the same thing, and they are close to each other but are not precisely the same. Let's presume they are close relatives, cousins, maybe. To me, arrogance is blindness to the real reason for one success. Overconfidence is thinking too highly of our abilities. Overconfidence is even more amplified when we have some illusion of control. That's why people prefer to pick the number on their lottery tickets rather than having them randomly selected. As if picking the numbers makes you more likely to win. Let's get this straight, I have nothing against confidence; in fact, confidence is a must. It helps you go through a rough times; it helps you cope better with fear and stress. The issue here is not with confidence but with overconfidence. Let me share a study* made in 1979 with clinically depressed patients. What you should know is that clinically depressed patients have no illusions about their abilities; in fact, it's this illusion that most of the time leads them to depression. For the study, non-depressed patients are put in a dark room with one light switch that works 75% of the time. Then clinically depressed patients are put in the same room with the same light switch that still works 75% of the time. Participants are given the task to open and close the light a certain number of times. Once the test was complete, most non-depressive participants claimed to have a relatively high level of control over the light. In contrast, the depressive ones claimed to have no control whatsoever. In fact, not a single participant had any control. This said, only the depressed ones were aware of it. Overconfidence.

It's the same thing when it comes to investment; I often tell new investors that the worst thing that can happen to you is being right the first time. It creates this false sense of control and fuels your overconfidence to a whole new level. It's like the classic scam from that pool movie with Tom Cruise, "The Color of Money." You first bet a small amount of money, lose miserably to build your opponent's overconfidence, raise the stakes and then completely obliterate them and collect big. I know this will sound strange, but losing the first time would have been in your best interest (overconfidence wise).

CASE STUDY (PART 7)

For a while now, my Slim investment has started to make me wonder whether or not I should keep making those impulsive investments. But then I remembered that although I only did this once before, it ended up being fantastic the last time. I will have faith in my abilities, trust my track record, and keep the course.

Dumb fool, last time was pure luck, and you know it. You don't have any abilities. Tom Cruise is about to get all your money...

EIGHTH TRAP: HYPERACTIVITY. (IMPATIENCE)

When the best thing to do is nothing at all...

A vast majority of today's investors seem to suffer from attention deficit and hyperactivity. 120... 120 is the average number of days that today's investor holds a position in his portfolio. As recently as 50 years ago, this number was more like 3,000. This means that today's investor chooses an investment based on the projected performance for the next 4 months, whereas in 1960, investors were investing for the next 100 months*. Why is this so? First, because we are impatient. Secondly, when things don't go our way, the last thing we want is to feel powerless in the face of the situation. Finally because, for most people, activity seems much better than inactivity, even if it is terrible.

A recent study* of soccer goalkeepers taking penalty shots demonstrates this trait. The researchers in the study analyzed 311 penalty shots in the world's top leagues and various significant championships. They found that, although as many shots are taken from the center of the net as from the right or left, goal-keepers dive to the right or left 94% of the time rather than staying in the center of the net. Even worse, the same success rate on shots from the center of the net is by far the highest (60%) of the three. When asked about this, the goalies said they would much rather dive in the wrong direction and be wrong than stand there in the middle of the net and look like they are doing nothing.

Remember this, just as professional soccer goalkeepers would do well to advocate inactivity from time to time, the seasoned investor must learn to stand tall in the storm from time to time and keep their focus on the horizon.

I'm giving you a 2 for 1 special this time with not one but 2 quotes from the Oracle from Omaha (Warren Buffett)

"The stock market is a tool to transfer money from the impatient to the patient."

"Holding cash is uncomfortable, but not as uncomfortable as doing something stupid."

— WARREN BUFFETT

CASE STUDY (PART 8)

You have to strike while the iron is hot. The new IPO may not have had the desired effect, but I've decided to be proactive this time rather than reactive. My new strategy is to buy each time the stock hits a new low, which will allow me to dilute my average price to such a low level that at the first significant rise. I would sell my entire position, hopefully with no losses.

> *Hyperactivity, the strategy put in place is in no way logical considering that the investment in the first place was not a good one. It may give a certain impression of control but, in fact, makes us even more vulnerable.*

NINTH TRAP: FOLLOWING THE HERD. (CONFORMIST)

The first experiment on social conformity was conducted by Jenness (1932). In his experiment, Jenness asked several candidates individually to estimate how many beans were in a bowl. He then combined all the candidates together and asked them to estimate once more the number of beans in the same bowl and then took the candidates back individually and offered them the opportunity, if they wished, to change their first estimate. Almost all subjects chose to revise their initial prediction to be closer to the one from the group.

Solomon Asch* (1951) took the analysis a step further when he developed an experiment in which he asked 8 subjects to identify the line on a card that was the same length as another line. Easy, right?

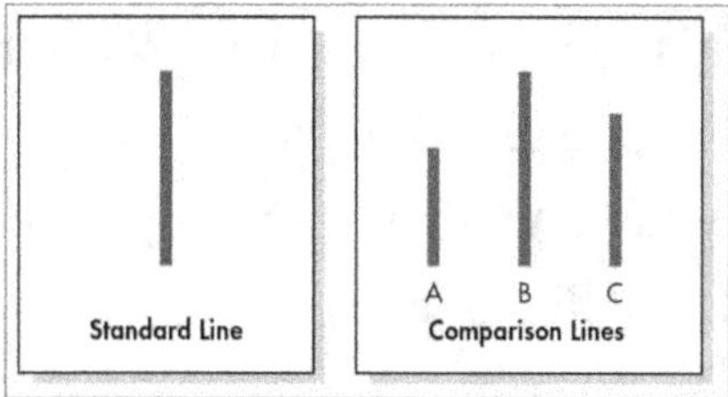

The only problem was that 7 of the 8 participants were actually part of the experiment and were asked to give the wrong answer to see if the actual subject would be influenced. In more than a third of the cases, the group managed to influence the real candidate even though the correct answer seemed obvious. This said, in this case, if only one other participant gave the correct answer, then only 5% of the actual subjects changed their answer.

Modern technology allows us to go even further. The same test was performed on candidates while magnetic imaging analyzed their brains. The results are fascinating. They show that not only going along with social norms create a pleasant situation in the subject, but the opposite stimulates the portion of the brain responsible for physical pain.

These experiences conclude that it is difficult to go against the grain. Going against social norms is not only unpleasant; it's painful. When it comes to investing, a large part of your success as an investor depends on your ability to form your own opinions and to be able, when necessary, to go against popular opinion. As Sir John Templeton so aptly put it: "It is impossible to outperform the majority unless you do things differently from the majority.

The idea here is not to make you a black sheep but to make you understand that it is essential to have your own independent opinion and to be able to stand behind your convictions even when the whole world disagrees.

~

CASE STUDY (PART 9)

A year has passed, and here I am again in the middle of Thanksgiving dinner eating my emotions (yes, again, the sugar pie). At the same time, my brother-in-law tells me that he sold his position in Slim just like his contacts and friends who had invested in the company like me. I tell him that it was my intention, too (I don't want to be that guy who doesn't understand when everyone else has understood). I sell my position the very next morning. Four hours later, I learn that Slim's stock is experiencing a dizzying rise following the announcement of the possible acquisition of the company by a giant in the pharmaceutical industry.

*I literally feel sick to my stomach, and this time, I
don't think it's because of the sugar pie.*

The good news is that now that you know the 9 most common pitfalls you will face, it is now possible to establish the DNA of the excellent investor: **open-minded** (pitfall #1), **lucid** (pitfall #2), **rational** (pitfall #3), **realistic** (pitfall #4), **focused** (pitfall #5), **humble** (pitfall #6), **modest** (pitfall#7), **patient** (pitfall #8) and occasionally **bold** (pitfall #9). I doubt very much that anyone has all these qualities simultaneously. The idea here is to be alert and aware of your own weaknesses. If patience is not your strong point? Beware of hyperactivity. Do you tend to get carried away by your good moves? Show a little more humility. You're easily convinced by a great story; remember that when it's too good to be true, it's too good to be true.

"IT'S NOT PERSONAL; ITS BUSINESS" / LEAVE THE HEART, BRING THE BRAIN

Emotions on your investment portfolio and business have the same impact as cancer has on your body. Looking for an excellent way to squander your wealth? I have two solutions for you:

1. Leave your brain at the door and let your heart make your financial decisions.
2. I leave you my address, and you send me a check. I will take care of the rest.

I know that money is emotional, but you should definitely not deal with it if you cannot detach yourself emotionally from it. It's easy to lose focus, so you should put mechanisms in place to protect yourself from yourself. Here are a few tips that I think will make you a better investor. And I'm telling you right away, don't feel bad if you recognize yourself in some of those common mistakes. Far be it from me, to claim of having never made those mistakes; in fact, I made all those mistakes at some point or another. How the heck do you think I learned all this stuff and got to become so good at what I do.

TIP #1: BUY LOW AND SELL HIGH

I don't think I'm teaching anyone anything if I tell you that the goal in investing is to buy low and sell high. I feel embarrassed to write this because it's so obvious. Still, it's inevitably the first concept to go out the window when emotion takes over from reason. I'm telling you, the only place in the world where people are constantly trying to buy high and sell low is in the financial markets. I can't even count the number of times a client has asked me to buy a stock because it just went up 30%, or a client has begged me to sell it because it just went down 10%.

It's December 22, 2017; I'm about to go on vacation for the holiday season, and, like at the end of each year, I consult Google Trends. This website permanently reports the most searched items on the Internet. For several months now, the number 1 research on the planet: "How do I buy Bitcoin with my credit card?". As if it weren't enough to buy a product with not only nebulous but purely speculative for $26,000 when it wasn't worth $800 just a year ago, financing this purchase with a credit card (at 26% interest) seems to be nothing less than the worst idea in the world.

A whole year had passed, and we are now on December 21, 2018, the number 1 search on the planet: "Fortnite". OK, but not far behind in 2nd place: "How to get rid of my Bitcoins?" Not surprisingly, Bitcoins aren't even worth $4,000 anymore, and many people just wish they had never heard of them in the first place. Just six months later, Bitcoins are worth $13,000.

PS: Those who thought it was a good idea in December 2017 to buy Bitcoins at $26,000 with their credit card and sell them by the end of 2018 have made an impressive one year return of -114%

TIP #2: INVEST WITH A PURPOSE.

Many people mistakenly think that the most challenging part of investing is finding the right stock. In reality, it is possible to make money with just about anything if you have the right strategy. Keep in mind that when you buy a stock, you buy a portion of a real company that you think is undervalued (if it is not undervalued, you may want to spend more time on rule #1). Before you even buy a stock, you should know your objective. Would you buy an old car to restore it and resell it for a profit without knowing its eventual resale value? It's the same with stocks. You don't buy stock to make money; you buy it because you want to make a 15%, 20, or 50% return. You don't start a recipe, thinking we'll see along the way if I have all the necessary ingredients to finish it. You don't go on a road trip without preparing an itinerary, and you wouldn't set out to build a house without first drawing up a plan. Investing with a purpose means having a clear idea of what you do, how you do it, and why.

At the risk of being blamed for my lack of originality, I, like many before me, will make you relive the nightmare that was Nortel Network. Everyone knows the story of Nortel, its spectacular rise from $10 to $120 to eventually end up at $0. Most people don't know that, globally, at the time of the crash, the average stock price for all Nortel holders was $17. This means that on average, Nortel holders posted, the day before the crash, a gain of +700%. Isn't greed one of the seven deadly sins?

I am convinced that no investor had the objective of making a return of 700% on day 1. Several people say: maybe, but imagine how much money I would have left on the table if I had exited at $34. I'm not too strong at math, but +100% is a lot better than -100% in my book. You want to continue enjoying the Nortel madness; no problem. Take out your profits every time you double your bet and keep your initial investment. This straight-forward little strategy would have allowed you to get out of the Nortel experience with a +600% return, even assuming that you lose your initial investment at the very end. Enough to make you an absolute urban legend.

TIP #3: "KNOW WHEN TO HOLD THEM; KNOW WHEN TO FOLD THEM! "

The hardest thing to do in my business is to sell. "I haven't lost until I've sold." I can't hear that one anymore. That's just a lousy loser's excuse.

NEWS FLASH: YOU WON'T ALWAYS BE RIGHT. I know it's not easy to admit that you're wrong, but no one likes the little

"Joe know-it-alls" who are never wrong. The home run hitter doesn't like to look foolish the 4 out of 5 times he gets struck out, and Sydney Crosby doesn't like looking ridiculous because he falls on his butt during a pre-game warm-up either. Excuse my language, but "SHIT HAPPENS". You need to be able to recognize when your plan, however great it may be, goes sideways. Don't let your ego (your emotions) get in the way, and know when it's time to move on to another call. The good news is: in my business if you're right 55% of the time, you're among the best. So contrary to what you may think, you don't look crazy at all when you're wrong. It's when you refuse to admit it that you look like a fool.

You may think it's easier to be disciplined when you're right, but I can promise you it's not. Letting go of your masterpiece, which makes you look like a real pro, is just as hard. You'd be surprised how many people tell me about their successes the way they tell me about their grandchildren. "Franck, why did you sell that title? It's been going up for the past two years, and worse, you did it to buy that thing that hasn't stopped falling for the past year? Do I really have to explain rule #1 to you again?

This could also be explained by what is called the endowment effect. An emotional bias leads an individual to attribute more value to a good that they possess than if they did not possess it. This phenomenon has been the subject of experiments by several researchers, notably Daniel Kahneman, a psychologist and economist and winner of the Nobel Prize in Economics in 2002. One of his experiments consisted of offering a coffee cup to a group of subjects and asking them how much they would be willing to sell it. The members of another group, who did not receive a cup, were asked how much they were willing to pay for the same coffee cup. The value of the coffee mug was significantly higher for the first group than for the second group, suggesting that owning the item increases its value. The endowment effect often manifests itself in everyday life. It is one of the reasons why your basement or attic is filled with completely useless and most likely worthless items. To avoid this kind of bias, rather than asking, "How much do I value this item?", it's better to ask, "If I hadn't owned it, how much would I be willing to buy it for?"

What is discipline? It's having a strategy and a plan and respecting it during the good and bad times. Have you ever heard the expression "It's not personal; it's business"? You would do well to remember it.

It may be because I've been lucky enough to not have many of those bad investments in my career that I remember this one, or maybe because it was the first one (and we never forget the first one). Still, I remember this one as if it was yesterday.

Chicago Bridge and Iron (CBI) on the NYSE. I was so optimistic about this one. The company was building heavy steel structures. We're talking bridge, baseball park, oil storage unit, ship, railroad, etc. They seemed to be involved in pretty much anything related to steel. I did my research, and the company's future seemed brighter than ever before. The company had just signed a huge contract to build major projects, including NFL Stadiums, Supertankers, and a couple of massive bridges. Nothing could seem to prevent this company from generating humongous growth. Nothing but cash flow.

Having so many massive projects simultaneously put a lot of pressure on their cash reserve and eventually forced the company to cut dividends and, by doing so, lost the favor of the public. One thing you need to know about the stock market is that a company's stock price on the market is a measure of popularity, not value. If a stock goes out of favor, there is really no limit to how low it can get. I could not believe that a company with so many significant contracts could default. But at some point, you must stop swimming against the tide and know when to fold it. No matter if it makes sense or not. That's precisely why I put a stop loss mechanism in place. So against my own desire, I've complied with my own rule and cut my loss in this case at -45% by selling my position. The company kept going down to reach -75% in value within a bit more than a year. The company got bought a year later for no premium by McDermott International (MDR), who filed for bankruptcy themselves three years later. Lesson learned.

TIP #4: PROTECT YOURSELF FROM YOURSELF.

Why tease the devil? You know you are predisposed to emotion, so why expose yourself to it unnecessarily. Meet Max. Max, a family man, works 70 hours a week and has no time to dwell on his investments. Max's strategy is to invest his entire portfolio in the TSX and review his performance yearly. Like everyone else, Max does not like losses and is satisfied 7 years out of 10 as his portfolio increases 7 times out of 10. Life is good.

Max is finally retired. His new "hobby"? He decides to follow his portfolio more closely. Max doesn't like what he sees, as his portfolio is up only 1 month out of 2. Worried, he starts tracking his portfolio every day and, to his dismay, realizes that things are getting worse and worse as his portfolio is now up only 1 day out of 3. It's time to panic.

Relax Max. There's nothing new here. Your portfolio has always had the same results. The TSX, over the past 30 years, has risen 70% of the time over a 12-month period, 50% of the time on a monthly basis, and only 29% of the time on a daily basis*. Teasing the devil.

Max has always had a certain discipline in the past, which has allowed him to achieve excellent results. Imagine that Max had, 30 years ago, a portfolio of $100,000. His lack of emotion would have allowed him to accumulate $527,913.94 30 years later.

Year	Price Start	Price End	Gains or Losses	Gains or Losses	Invested
1985	2595.15	2842.96	247.81	9.55%	$ 109,548.97
1986	2842.96	3348.9	505.94	17.80%	$ 129,044.56
1987	3348.9	3160.05	-188.85	-5.64%	$ 121,767.53
1988	3160.05	3389.99	229.94	7.28%	$ 130,627.90
1989	3389.99	3969.79	579.8	17.10%	$ 152,965.27
1990	3969.79	3256.75	-713.04	-17.96%	$ 125,492.71
1991	3256.75	3512.36	255.61	7.85%	$ 135,343.89
1992	3512.36	3350.44	-161.92	-4.61%	$ 129,104.53
1993	3350.44	4321.43	970.99	28.98%	$ 166,519.03
1994	4321.43	4213.61	-107.82	-2.50%	$ 162,356.05
1995	4213.61	4713.54	499.93	11.86%	$ 181,611.48
1996	4713.54	5927.03	1213.49	25.74%	$ 228,358.28
1997	5927.03	6699.44	772.41	13.03%	$ 258,113.36
1998	6699.44	6485.94	-213.5	-3.19%	$ 249,879.54
1999	6485.94	8413.75	1927.81	29.72%	$ 324,143.74
2000	8413.75	8933.68	519.93	6.18%	$ 344,175.83
2001	8933.68	7688.41	-1245.27	-13.94%	$ 296,197.72
2002	7688.41	6614.54	-1073.87	-13.97%	$ 254,818.90
2003	6614.54	8220.89	1606.35	24.29%	$ 316,714.41
2004	8220.89	9246.65	1025.76	12.48%	$ 356,240.36
2005	9246.65	11272.26	2025.61	21.91%	$ 434,292.63
2006	11272.26	12908.39	1636.13	14.51%	$ 497,308.49
2007	12908.39	13833.06	924.67	7.16%	$ 532,915.78
2008	13833.06	8987.7	-4845.36	-35.03%	$ 346,235.38
2009	8987.7	11746.11	2758.41	30.69%	$ 452,495.02
2010	11746.11	13443.22	1697.11	14.45%	$ 517,880.55
2011	13443.22	11955.09	-1488.13	-11.07%	$ 460,551.17
2012	11955.09	12433.53	478.44	4.00%	$ 478,973.22
2013	12433.53	13621.55	1188.02	9.55%	$ 524,715.16
2014	13621.55	14632.44	1010.89	7.42%	$ 563,655.61
2015	14632.44	13704.59	-927.85	-6.34%	**$ 527,913.94**

Now imagine that Max had an emotional response to market fluctuations, i.e., that he exited the market after every down year and re-entered the market after every up year. Well, Max's portfolio would be worth $167,753.88 today, or 3 times less.

Year	Price Start	Price End	Gains or Losses	Gains or Losses	Invested	Emotional
1985	2595.15	2842.96	247.81	9.55%	$ 109,548.97	$ 109,548.97
1986	2842.96	3348.9	505.94	17.80%	$ 129,044.56	$ 129,044.56
1987	3348.9	3160.05	-188.85	-5.64%	$ 121,767.53	$ 121,767.53
1988	3160.05	3389.99	229.94	7.28%	$ 130,627.90	$ 121,767.53
1989	3389.99	3969.79	579.8	17.10%	$ 152,965.27	$ 142,589.78
1990	3969.79	3256.75	-713.04	-17.96%	$ 125,492.71	$ 116,980.65
1991	3256.75	3512.36	255.61	7.85%	$ 135,343.89	$ 116,980.65
1992	3512.36	3350.44	-161.92	-4.61%	$ 129,104.53	$ 111,587.84
1993	3350.44	4321.43	970.99	28.98%	$ 166,519.03	$ 111,587.84
1994	4321.43	4213.61	-107.82	-2.50%	$ 162,356.05	$ 108,798.15
1995	4213.61	4713.54	499.93	11.86%	$ 181,611.48	$ 108,798.15
1996	4713.54	5927.03	1213.49	25.74%	$ 228,358.28	$ 136,802.79
1997	5927.03	6699.44	772.41	13.03%	$ 258,113.36	$ 154,628.19
1998	6699.44	6485.94	-213.5	-3.19%	$ 249,879.54	$ 149,695.55
1999	6485.94	8413.75	1927.81	29.72%	$ 324,143.74	$ 149,695.55
2000	8413.75	8933.68	519.93	6.18%	$ 344,175.83	$ 158,946.74
2001	8933.68	7688.41	-1245.27	-13.94%	$ 296,197.72	$ 136,789.56
2002	7688.41	6614.54	-1073.87	-13.97%	$ 254,818.90	$ 136,789.56
2003	6614.54	8220.89	1606.35	24.29%	$ 316,714.41	$ 136,789.56
2004	8220.89	9246.65	1025.76	12.48%	$ 356,240.36	$ 153,860.90
2005	9246.65	11272.26	2025.61	21.91%	$ 434,292.63	$ 187,571.83
2006	11272.26	12908.39	1636.13	14.51%	$ 497,308.49	$ 214,788.50
2007	12908.39	13833.06	924.67	7.16%	$ 532,915.78	$ 230,167.35
2008	13833.06	8987.7	-4845.36	-35.03%	$ 346,235.38	$ 149,539.73
2009	8987.7	11746.11	2758.41	30.69%	$ 452,495.02	$ 149,539.73
2010	11746.11	13443.22	1697.11	14.45%	$ 517,880.55	$ 171,148.22
2011	13443.22	11955.09	-1488.13	-11.07%	$ 460,551.17	$ 152,202.11
2012	11955.09	12433.53	478.44	4.00%	$ 478,973.22	$ 152,202.11
2013	12433.53	13621.55	1188.02	9.55%	$ 524,715.16	$ 166,737.41
2014	13621.55	14632.44	1010.89	7.42%	$ 563,655.61	$ 179,111.42
2015	14632.44	13704.59	-927.85	-6.34%	$ 527,913.94	**$ 167,753.88**

-68.22%

Some Fund companies did an analysis to identify who was their best-performing investor for the period 2003-2013. The answer: THE DEAD. Ironically, it was indeed the forgotten or frozen estate accounts that performed the best over the period in question. Conclusion: leave the emotions at the door, and your portfolio will be much better off.

TIP #5: THE PAST IS NO GUARANTEE OF THE FUTURE.

If I offered you to play a game of 20 rounds of heads or tails with me (with a coin, all that is legal, of course) and that each time you are wrong, it will cost you 1$ while each time you are right, I will give you 2.50$. If you let SHERLOCK work here, you understand that you would be crazy not to play each of the 20 rounds. Indeed, the amount I give you in case of a win is much more favorable than your cost if you lose.

SHERLOCK'S PROCESS OF REFLECTION: THE PROBABILITY OF winning a flip coin is 50%. This means that by playing all 20 rounds of the game, I'm expecting to win 10 rounds and lose the other 10. By winning 10 rounds at 2.50$ per win, I should expect to get out of the game with 25$ (10 X 2.50$ = 25$). In fact, mathematically, your $20 will be worth more in 87% of cases, and you would lose money in only 13% of cases (if you play all the "rounds").

JOE'S PROCESS OF REFLECTION: YEAH, GAMBLING, LET'S DO this...

SOME RESEARCHERS* HAVE DONE THE EXERCISE AND OBSERVED that only 58% of the individuals played every round. Even worse, only 40% of the individuals continued to play after a loss. It is also interesting to note that the more the game progressed, the worse the individuals' ability to make rational decisions. It's almost as if JOE took over after a while.

You may have drawn a parallel here with our stock markets. Just like in my game, when the markets are down, and everything is selling at a discount, fear (JOE) very often prevents people from doing what makes sense, especially if those same people have suffered losses before. In fact, the longer investors stay in this loss zone, the less focused they are. It's always funny to hear investors talk in the middle of a crash as if the markets will never go up again. After 200 years and a good thirty crashes, you would think people would have finally understood... But obviously, this is not the case... I think it's time for another famous quote from Mr. Buffett. Yes, it's time.

"In a time of crisis, we learn a lot in the short term, a little less in midterm and nothing else in the long term."

Warren Buffett

TIP #6: STAY RATIONAL.

I will never forget, a few years ago, a client called me in a panic because her portfolio dropped 1% last month. During our conversation, she tells me that according to her calculations, at the current rate, she will lose 12% this year. I felt at the moment like answering my client not to worry because her portfolio is going up 1% today, which means that at the current rate, she's going to make 250% this year, but I remember that it's precisely why this client pays me in the first place. To offer her a rational and calm path when she feels emotional and nervous.

It's funny; a few years ago, I was helping my son with his math homework. "Louis plays marbles. At the start of the day, he had 10 marbles. He wins 10 more during the first break and then loses 5 over lunch break. How many marbles does Louis now have from where he started?" My little 8-year-old man looks at me and says, "Bah, that's too easy! That's 5 marbles more. Wow! I tell myself my son is an absolute genius (I'm not biased at all here). Indeed my 8-year-old son has understood what millions of investors of all ages, spread over almost any continent, have not yet understood. If you start your year with a portfolio of $100,000, gain $20,000 after 6 months, and then lose $10,000 in the next 6 months and well at the end of the year, you have made a profit of $10,000. You didn't lose $10,000. It sounds simple, but it's inescapable: just about any investor who sees his portfolio fluctuate uses the peak as a reference point. It's another emotional bias that causes us to lose our sanity. Worse yet, we don't always make this mistake; we just do it when it's convenient. You go to the casino with $100 to raise your winnings to $250 before you finally lose it all (surprise, surprise). At the end of the night, you don't say your night cost you $250; you say it cost you $100. Or, you go on a diet, lose 20 pounds in the first 3 months, and gain 5 pounds back in the 4th month. You're not going to brag to your friends about gaining 5 pounds but losing 15.

I've been busting your chops for three chapters now about how screwed up, vulnerable, and pathetic we are when it comes to talking about investing. You may wonder if this book is really meant to help you or just to demoralize you. But trust me, I have a good reason. You see, it is only by being aware of your shortcomings and vulnerability that you can avoid the pitfalls that will inevitably come your way.

Or, as the honorable Yoda would say: "HUMM of your shortcomings and vulnerability, aware you must be if avoid the traps you want."

TIME CAN BE YOUR FRIEND OR YOUR FOE / THE ART OF DOING NOTHING

TIME IS KEY TO ACCUMULATING A HUGE AMOUNT OF MONEY.

(Wait. I can do better)

TIME IS KEY TO ACCUMULATING HUGE AMOUNT OF MONEY.

(It's almost there, but I think maybe if I do:)

TIME IS THE KEY TO ACCUMULATING A HUGE AMOUNT OF MONEY.

(I think you've got it…)

OK, FIRST OF ALL, I WANT TO WARN YOU THAT THE NEXT section will have some mathematical content. This is unfortunately unavoidable to cover the topic of this chapter but have no fear. I will keep it as simple as possible. So, let's get to it.

Meet Max and Julie, who have just given birth to little Olivier. Unfortunately, shortly after, Olivier's grandfather passed away and left him the sum of $10,000 that Max and Julie decided to invest in an account for Olivier.

Olivier grew up with minimal financial discipline, living in the moment without much concern for his old age. He is not aware of the existence of this account.

Now, let me introduce you to Marco. Marco was fortunate enough to benefit from his grandfather for a long time, but he never received an inheritance. That being said, Marco has shown excellent discipline, and at the age of 25, he started saving $3000 for his retirement. Marco maintains this discipline throughout his life. He adds $3,000 to his savings account every year until his 60th birthday.

At age 60, Marco invested 10.8 times more capital in his account than Olivier ($108,000 vs. $10,000). Who do you think will be wealthier at age 60, Marco or Olivier?

If you answered Marco, then, unfortunately, you are wrong. Not only will Olivier have more capital at his disposal, but he will have 2.5 times more than Marco ($1,918,741 vs. $772,128).

OLIVIER	BEGIN	DEPOSIT	RETURN	END
0	$0	$10,000	$900	$10,900
1	$10,900	$0	$981	$11,881
2	$11,881	$0	$1,069	$12,950
3	$12,950	$0	$1,166	$14,116
4	$14,116	$0	$1,270	$15,386
5	$15,386	$0	$1,385	$16,771
6	$16,771	$0	$1,509	$18,280
7	$18,280	$0	$1,645	$19,926
8	$19,926	$0	$1,793	$21,719
9	$21,719	$0	$1,955	$23,674
10	$23,674	$0	$2,131	$25,804
11	$25,804	$0	$2,322	$28,127
12	$28,127	$0	$2,531	$30,658
13	$30,658	$0	$2,759	$33,417
14	$33,417	$0	$3,008	$36,425
15	$36,425	$0	$3,278	$39,703
16	$39,703	$0	$3,573	$43,276
17	$43,276	$0	$3,895	$47,171
18	$47,171	$0	$4,245	$51,417
19	$51,417	$0	$4,627	$56,044
20	$56,044	$0	$5,044	$61,088
21	$61,088	$0	$5,498	$66,586
22	$66,586	$0	$5,993	$72,579
23	$72,579	$0	$6,532	$79,111
24	$79,111	$0	$7,120	$86,231
25	$86,231	$0	$7,761	$93,992
26	$93,992	$0	$8,459	$102,451
27	$102,451	$0	$9,221	$111,671
28	$111,671	$0	$10,050	$121,722
29	$121,722	$0	$10,955	$132,677
30	$132,677	$0	$11,941	$144,618
31	$144,618	$0	$13,016	$157,633
32	$157,633	$0	$14,187	$171,820
33	$171,820	$0	$15,464	$187,284
34	$187,284	$0	$16,856	$204,140
35	$204,140	$0	$18,373	$222,512
36	$222,512	$0	$20,026	$242,538
37	$242,538	$0	$21,828	$264,367
38	$264,367	$0	$23,793	$288,160
39	$288,160	$0	$25,934	$314,094
40	$314,094	$0	$28,268	$342,363
41	$342,363	$0	$30,813	$373,175
42	$373,175	$0	$33,586	$406,761
43	$406,761	$0	$36,608	$443,370
44	$443,370	$0	$39,903	$483,273
45	$483,273	$0	$43,495	$526,767
46	$526,767	$0	$47,409	$574,176
47	$574,176	$0	$51,676	$625,852
48	$625,852	$0	$56,327	$682,179
49	$682,179	$0	$61,396	$743,575
50	$743,575	$0	$66,922	$810,497
51	$810,497	$0	$72,945	$883,442
52	$883,442	$0	$79,510	$962,951
53	$962,951	$0	$86,666	$1,049,617
54	$1,049,617	$0	$94,466	$1,144,083
55	$1,144,083	$0	$102,967	$1,247,050
56	$1,247,050	$0	$112,235	$1,359,285
57	$1,359,285	$0	$122,336	$1,481,620
58	$1,481,620	$0	$133,346	$1,614,966
59	$1,614,966	$0	$145,347	$1,760,313
60	$1,760,313	$0	$158,428	$1,918,741

MARCO	BEGIN	DEPOSIT	RETURN	END
0	$0	$0	$0	$0
1	$0	$0	$0	$0
2	$0	$0	$0	$0
3	$0	$0	$0	$0
4	$0	$0	$0	$0
5	$0	$0	$0	$0
6	$0	$0	$0	$0
7	$0	$0	$0	$0
8	$0	$0	$0	$0
9	$0	$0	$0	$0
10	$0	$0	$0	$0
11	$0	$0	$0	$0
12	$0	$0	$0	$0
13	$0	$0	$0	$0
14	$0	$0	$0	$0
15	$0	$0	$0	$0
16	$0	$0	$0	$0
17	$0	$0	$0	$0
18	$0	$0	$0	$0
19	$0	$0	$0	$0
20	$0	$0	$0	$0
21	$0	$0	$0	$0
22	$0	$0	$0	$0
23	$0	$0	$0	$0
24	$0	$0	$0	$0
25	$0	$3,000	$270	$3,270
26	$3,270	$3,000	$564	$6,834
27	$6,834	$3,000	$885	$10,719
28	$10,719	$3,000	$1,235	$14,954
29	$14,954	$3,000	$1,616	$19,570
30	$19,570	$3,000	$2,031	$24,601
31	$24,601	$3,000	$2,484	$30,085
32	$30,085	$3,000	$2,978	$36,063
33	$36,063	$3,000	$3,516	$42,579
34	$42,579	$3,000	$4,102	$49,681
35	$49,681	$3,000	$4,741	$57,422
36	$57,422	$3,000	$5,438	$65,860
37	$65,860	$3,000	$6,197	$75,058
38	$75,058	$3,000	$7,025	$85,083
39	$85,083	$3,000	$7,927	$96,010
40	$96,010	$3,000	$8,911	$107,921
41	$107,921	$3,000	$9,983	$120,904
42	$120,904	$3,000	$11,151	$135,055
43	$135,055	$3,000	$12,425	$150,480
44	$150,480	$3,000	$13,813	$167,294
45	$167,294	$3,000	$15,326	$185,620
46	$185,620	$3,000	$16,976	$205,596
47	$205,596	$3,000	$18,774	$227,369
48	$227,369	$3,000	$20,733	$251,103
49	$251,103	$3,000	$22,869	$276,972
50	$276,972	$3,000	$25,197	$305,169
51	$305,169	$3,000	$27,735	$335,905
52	$335,905	$3,000	$30,501	$369,406
53	$369,406	$3,000	$33,517	$405,923
54	$405,923	$3,000	$36,803	$445,726
55	$445,726	$3,000	$40,385	$489,111
56	$489,111	$3,000	$44,290	$536,401
57	$536,401	$3,000	$48,546	$587,947
58	$587,947	$3,000	$53,185	$644,132
59	$644,132	$3,000	$58,242	$705,374
60	$705,374	$3,000	$63,754	$772,128

In fact, if Olivier's inheritance had been only $4000 or if Olivier's annual return would have been 18% lower than Marco's (7.38% instead of 9%). Olivier would have accumulated, in the end, the same amount as Marco. In fact, Marco would have had to save $7,458 per year for 35 years for a total of $261,030 (26 times more than Olivier) to reach the same amount at age 60.

Accepting this concept, for some, is a bit like going through the emotional phases linked to the announcement of bad news. First, there is:

1. Denial: this is not possible; there must be a mistake;
2. Anger: it is unfair, I object;
3. Bargaining: there is undoubtedly something to be done;
4. Depression: I'm screwed; I'm already 40;
5. Acceptance: what's done is done. What's plan B?

You are free to linger in one of the first 4 phases if you want, but the following section is for those of you who have reached phase 5: Acceptance. Those who have understood that 40 years old may not be as good as 25 or 15 years old, but it is still better than 50 years old...

Albert Einstein said, "Compound interest is the most powerful force in our universe." Too many people mistakenly believe that wealthy people have necessarily inherited an obscene amount of money, won the lottery, or founded a multinational corporation. You would fall off your chair if you knew where that wealth really came from.

What, in the name of God, is compound interest? Compound interest is nothing more than the interest you make on your interest. If I take the example of Olivier and Marco and if Olivier makes a return of 9% per year, then his gain at the end of the first year will be $900.

AGE OLIVIER	BEGIN	DEPOSIT	INTERESTS	COMPOUND INTEREST	FINAL	RETURN ON INITIAL INVESTMENT
0	$0	$10,000	$900	$0	$10,900	9.00%

That said, the magic begins in year 2 when the compound interest starts. As in year 1, Olivier will earn $900 on his $10,000 (9% X 10,000 = $900) but will also earn a *little extra* as he will also generate $81 on the earnings of year 1 (9% X $900 = $81). For a grand total by the end of year 2 of 981$

AGE OLIVIER	BEGIN	DEPOSIT	INTERESTS	COMPOUND INTEREST	FINAL	RETURN ON INITIAL INVESTMENT
0	$0	$10,000	$900	$0	$10,900	9.00%
1	$10,900	$0	$900	$81	$11,881	9.81%

Olivier's actual return on his initial investment for this year is 9.81% ($981 on $10,000). Wow! 0.81% more, you might say... But wait a minute because the magic is just beginning. What happens if I "Fast Forward" to when Olivier turns 25?

AGE OLIVIER	BEGIN	DEPOSIT	INTERESTS	COMPOUND INTEREST	FINAL	RETURN ON INITIAL INVESTMENT
0	$0	$10,000	$900	$0	$10,900	9.00%
1	$10,900	$0	$900	$81	$11,881	9.81%
2	$11,881	$0	$900	$169	$12,950	10.69%
3	$12,950	$0	$900	$266	$14,116	11.66%
4	$14,116	$0	$900	$370	$15,386	12.70%
5	$15,386	$0	$900	$485	$16,771	13.85%
6	$16,771	$0	$900	$609	$18,280	15.09%
7	$18,280	$0	$900	$745	$19,926	16.45%
8	$19,926	$0	$900	$893	$21,719	17.93%
9	$21,719	$0	$900	$1,055	$23,674	19.55%
10	$23,674	$0	$900	$1,231	$25,804	21.31%
11	$25,804	$0	$900	$1,422	$28,127	23.22%
12	$28,127	$0	$900	$1,631	$30,658	25.31%
13	$30,658	$0	$900	$1,859	$33,417	27.59%
14	$33,417	$0	$900	$2,108	$36,425	30.08%
15	$36,425	$0	$900	$2,378	$39,703	32.78%
16	$39,703	$0	$900	$2,673	$43,276	35.73%
17	$43,276	$0	$900	$2,995	$47,171	38.95%
18	$47,171	$0	$900	$3,345	$51,417	42.45%
19	$51,417	$0	$900	$3,727	$56,044	46.27%
20	$56,044	$0	$900	$4,144	$61,088	50.44%
21	$61,088	$0	$900	$4,598	$66,586	54.98%
22	$66,586	$0	$900	$5,093	$72,579	59.93%
23	$72,579	$0	$900	$5,632	$79,111	65.32%
24	$79,111	$0	$900	$6,220	$86,231	71.20%
25	$86,231	$0	$900	$6,861	$93,992	77.61%

On his 25th birthday, Olivier still makes his original 900$ (9% of 10,000$) but now also makes an extra 6,871$ of interest on its interest for a total return that year of 7,761$ or a 77.61% return on his initial investment. <u>Not bad, not bad at all.</u>

I don't know if you've noticed, but when Marco starts depositing $3,000 a year into his account, Olivier's compound interest (remember the *little extra*) adds $6,861 to his. Of course, Marco will never catch up to Olivier. But there's more…

If we fast forward to age 60, Olivier's total return represents a whopping 1584% return on the initial investment. The interest on the interest now generates $157,528 of *extra money* per year. If you are one of those skeptics still in the denial phase (phase 1), imagine if Olivier had the "bright idea" to withdraw his profits from his account every year. Well, Olivier would have collected a grand total of $54,000 in earnings ($900 X 60 years = $54,000) but would have lost his little extras for a total of **$1,854,741** (I'll spare you the math but trust me, it's the correct number).

AGE OLIVIER	BEGIN	DEPOSIT	INTERESTS	COMPOUND INTEREST	FINAL	RETURN ON INITIAL INVESTMENT
0	$0	$10,000	$900	$0	$10,900	9.00%
1	$10,900	$0	$900	$81	$11,881	9.81%
2	$11,881	$0	$900	$169	$12,950	10.69%
3	$12,950	$0	$900	$266	$14,116	11.66%
4	$14,116	$0	$900	$370	$15,386	12.70%
5	$15,386	$0	$900	$485	$16,771	13.85%
6	$16,771	$0	$900	$609	$18,280	15.09%
7	$18,280	$0	$900	$745	$19,926	16.45%
8	$19,926	$0	$900	$893	$21,719	17.93%
9	$21,719	$0	$900	$1,055	$23,674	19.55%
10	$23,674	$0	$900	$1,231	$25,804	21.31%
11	$25,804	$0	$900	$1,422	$28,127	23.22%
12	$28,127	$0	$900	$1,631	$30,658	25.31%
13	$30,658	$0	$900	$1,859	$33,417	27.59%
14	$33,417	$0	$900	$2,108	$36,425	30.08%
15	$36,425	$0	$900	$2,378	$39,703	32.78%
16	$39,703	$0	$900	$2,673	$43,276	35.73%
17	$43,276	$0	$900	$2,995	$47,171	38.95%
18	$47,171	$0	$900	$3,345	$51,417	42.45%
19	$51,417	$0	$900	$3,727	$56,044	46.27%
20	$56,044	$0	$900	$4,144	$61,088	50.44%
21	$61,088	$0	$900	$4,598	$66,586	54.98%
22	$66,586	$0	$900	$5,093	$72,579	59.93%
23	$72,579	$0	$900	$5,632	$79,111	65.32%
24	$79,111	$0	$900	$6,220	$86,231	71.20%
25	$86,231	$0	$900	$6,861	$93,992	77.61%
26	$93,992	$0	$900	$7,559	$102,451	84.59%
27	$102,451	$0	$900	$8,321	$111,671	92.21%
28	$111,671	$0	$900	$9,150	$121,722	100.50%
29	$121,722	$0	$900	$10,055	$132,677	109.55%
30	$132,677	$0	$900	$11,041	$144,618	119.41%
31	$144,618	$0	$900	$12,116	$157,633	130.16%
32	$157,633	$0	$900	$13,287	$171,820	141.87%
33	$171,820	$0	$900	$14,564	$187,284	154.64%
34	$187,284	$0	$900	$15,956	$204,140	168.56%
35	$204,140	$0	$900	$17,473	$222,512	183.73%
36	$222,512	$0	$900	$19,126	$242,538	200.26%
37	$242,538	$0	$900	$20,928	$264,367	218.28%
38	$264,367	$0	$900	$22,893	$288,160	237.93%
39	$288,160	$0	$900	$25,034	$314,094	259.34%
40	$314,094	$0	$900	$27,368	$342,363	282.68%
41	$342,363	$0	$900	$29,913	$373,175	308.13%
42	$373,175	$0	$900	$32,686	$406,761	335.86%
43	$406,761	$0	$900	$35,708	$443,370	366.08%
44	$443,370	$0	$900	$39,003	$483,273	399.03%
45	$483,273	$0	$900	$42,595	$526,767	434.95%
46	$526,767	$0	$900	$46,509	$574,176	474.09%
47	$574,176	$0	$900	$50,776	$625,852	516.76%
48	$625,852	$0	$900	$55,427	$682,179	563.27%
49	$682,179	$0	$900	$60,496	$743,575	613.96%
50	$743,575	$0	$900	$66,022	$810,497	669.22%
51	$810,497	$0	$900	$72,045	$883,442	729.45%
52	$883,442	$0	$900	$78,610	$962,951	795.10%
53	$962,951	$0	$900	$85,766	$1,049,617	866.66%
54	$1,049,617	$0	$900	$93,566	$1,144,083	944.66%
55	$1,144,083	$0	$900	$102,067	$1,247,050	1029.67%
56	$1,247,050	$0	$900	$111,335	$1,359,285	1122.35%
57	$1,359,285	$0	$900	$121,436	$1,481,620	1223.36%
58	$1,481,620	$0	$900	$132,446	$1,614,966	1333.46%
59	$1,614,966	$0	$900	$144,447	$1,760,313	1453.47%
60	$1,760,313	$0	$900	$157,528	$1,918,741	1584.28%

Not convinced yet? Let me tell you a tale I came across not so long ago that genuinely reflects the true power of compounded interest. In this story, a wealthy old man nearing the end of his days summoned his twin sons to his bedside to discuss their inheritance. The old man told both his sons that he would gift them each a briefcase containing either 1 million dollars or a briefcase containing nothing but a shiny penny. This gift however, came with one condition - the briefcase will remain under his butler's care for one entire month in order to give his sons time to think about how they were to use this money. In addition, if they were to choose the million-dollar briefcase, they may, if they wished, draw against it as credit with his bank. If they were to choose the penny briefcase, they can also draw against it, however, for every day they chose to leave the penny's line of credit untouched, his butler has been instructed to double the content of the briefcase until the 31st day of the month. The old man instructed his sons to reflect upon his proposal and to return the following day with their decision. The next morning, the first son arrived early and chose the penny briefcase. The second son, having partied all night arrived much later and informed his father that he chose the million-dollar briefcase. The second son had a plan - 1 million dollars is great, but it's not grand. He decided to borrow at the bank using the million dollars as collateral; hire a team of the sharpest investment experts he could find; use leverage, option and short selling strategies, that would allow him to grow his million fast as possible. Two weeks later, the second son met with his brother to find out how his brother's million dollar strategy was doing, only to find out, to his astonishment, that his brother had turned down the million-dollar briefcase and had opted instead for the the penny briefcase. He couldn't believe how foolish his brother was to have chosen the penny briefcase. He asks his brother how much he had in his briefcase. His brother replies that he has 81.92$. He is dumbfounded – 81.92$!!! What a fool his brother is. He tells his brother that in his briefcase, he's already at 1,250,000$. He tries to assure his brother that it may not be too late and that he should go see their father and to beg him to allow him to swap his penny briefcase for the million-dollar briefcase. He tells his brother, "You need to spend money to make money" and that this was the lesson that their father wanted them to understand. His brother refused and wouldn't hear of it. That same night the old man died peacefully in his sleep. The third week ended, and the two brothers met for lunch once again. The son who had chosen the million-dollar briefcase was curious and asked his brother how his

collection of pennies were coming along? To his amazement, his brother replied that he was now at 10,485.76$. On the morning of day 31, the bank director approached the son with the million-dollar briefcase with some bad news - the market had gone soft in the last week of the month, and because of margin calls, options expiring, and short selling on the wrong side, he was going to end up losing more the 500K. In fact, after fees, he would be left with just a little short of 300k. As sad as he was, the second son tried to console himself by convincing himself that that at least he's not ending up with pennies. That, of course, was before he found out that his brother had just received a briefcase with 10 million 737 thousand 418 dollars and 24 shiny pennies! That's the power of compounded interest (not sure of the math, check the table below):

day 1	$0.01	day 12	$20.48	day 22	$20,971.52
day 2	$0.02	day 13	$40.96	day 23	$41,943.04
day 3	$0.04	day 14	$81.92	day 24	$83,886.08
day 4	$0.08	day 15	$163.84	day 25	$167,772.16
day 5	$0.16	day 16	$327.68	day 26	$335,544.32
day 6	$0.32	day 17	$655.36	day 27	$671,088.64
day 7	$0.64	day 18	$1,310.72	day 28	$1,342,177.28
day 8	$1.28	day 19	$2,621.44	day 29	$2,684,354.56
day 9	$2.56	day 20	$5,242.88	day 30	$5,368,709.12
day 10	$5.12	day 21	$10,485.76	day 31	$10,737,418.24
day 11	$10.24				

I HOPE I HAVE SUCCEEDED IN CONVINCING YOU THAT THE KEY TO accumulating large sums is to maximize your compounded interest as much as possible. How to do it?

1. Start as soon as possible.
2. Don't touch your winnings until the end.

Now, I understand the reality of life. At 18, you have no money. At 25, it's student loans. At 30, the first house. At 35, kids. And at 40, it's depression because time is no longer your friend. The point here is that when time is your friend, **"a little goes a long way."** Another book I like: The Automatic Millionaire by David Bach, illustrates this concept wonderfully with his *Latte factor.* You are wondering what is the *Latte Factor?* Well, let me introduce you to David, 20 years old, who, every morning on his way to work, stops at Starbucks to get his traditional Double Double Mocha Latte with the whole package (chocolate, whipped cream, colored sugar, and the little cinnamon stick please). All for the modest sum of 5.95$. David is not really a morning person and is frankly not approachable without his coffee, so there is no way anyone would ask David to eliminate his coffee from his morning routine. But imagine David settling for a simple Mocha Latte (no whipped cream, colored sugar, or little cinnamon stick) at $3.95 and save his small savings of $2 in his piggy bank every day and move the content of that piggy bank by the end of the year (250 days of work X $2 per day = $500/year). If David continues this little merry-go-round until he retires at age 65. David will have saved $20,000 ($500/year X 40 years). Better yet, if David took the time to invest the amount in question to benefit from the accumulated interest (you can see me coming with my big shoes), David would have accumulated an extra $318,755 (in addition to reducing his daily calorific consumption by about 1,000,000 calories).

AGE	INITIAL VALUE	DEPOSIT	RETURNS	FINAL VALUE
20	$ -	$ 500.00	$ 45.00	$ 545.00
21	$ 545.00	$ 500.00	$ 94.05	$ 1,139.05
22	$ 1,139.05	$ 501.00	$ 147.60	$ 1,787.65
23	$ 1,787.65	$ 502.00	$ 206.07	$ 2,495.72
24	$ 2,495.72	$ 503.00	$ 269.89	$ 3,268.61
25	$ 3,268.61	$ 504.00	$ 339.53	$ 4,112.14
26	$ 4,112.14	$ 505.00	$ 415.54	$ 5,032.69
27	$ 5,032.69	$ 506.00	$ 498.48	$ 6,037.17
28	$ 6,037.17	$ 507.00	$ 588.98	$ 7,133.14
29	$ 7,133.14	$ 508.00	$ 687.70	$ 8,328.85
30	$ 8,328.85	$ 509.00	$ 795.41	$ 9,633.25
31	$ 9,633.25	$ 510.00	$ 912.89	$ 11,056.14
32	$ 11,056.14	$ 511.00	$ 1,041.04	$ 12,608.19
33	$ 12,608.19	$ 512.00	$ 1,180.82	$ 14,301.00
34	$ 14,301.00	$ 513.00	$ 1,333.26	$ 16,147.27
35	$ 16,147.27	$ 514.00	$ 1,499.51	$ 18,160.78
36	$ 18,160.78	$ 515.00	$ 1,680.82	$ 20,356.60
37	$ 20,356.60	$ 516.00	$ 1,878.53	$ 22,751.13
38	$ 22,751.13	$ 517.00	$ 2,094.13	$ 25,362.26
39	$ 25,362.26	$ 518.00	$ 2,329.22	$ 28,209.49
40	$ 28,209.49	$ 519.00	$ 2,585.56	$ 31,314.05
41	$ 31,314.05	$ 520.00	$ 2,865.06	$ 34,699.12
42	$ 34,699.12	$ 521.00	$ 3,169.81	$ 38,389.93
43	$ 38,389.93	$ 522.00	$ 3,502.07	$ 42,414.00
44	$ 42,414.00	$ 523.00	$ 3,864.33	$ 46,801.33
45	$ 46,801.33	$ 524.00	$ 4,259.28	$ 51,584.61
46	$ 51,584.61	$ 525.00	$ 4,689.87	$ 56,799.48
47	$ 56,799.48	$ 526.00	$ 5,159.29	$ 62,484.77
48	$ 62,484.77	$ 527.00	$ 5,671.06	$ 68,682.83
49	$ 68,682.83	$ 528.00	$ 6,228.97	$ 75,439.80
50	$ 75,439.80	$ 529.00	$ 6,837.19	$ 82,806.00
51	$ 82,806.00	$ 530.00	$ 7,500.24	$ 90,836.24
52	$ 90,836.24	$ 531.00	$ 8,223.05	$ 99,590.29
53	$ 99,590.29	$ 532.00	$ 9,011.01	$ 109,133.29
54	$ 109,133.29	$ 533.00	$ 9,869.97	$ 119,536.26
55	$ 119,536.26	$ 534.00	$ 10,806.32	$ 130,876.58
56	$ 130,876.58	$ 535.00	$ 11,827.04	$ 143,238.62
57	$ 143,238.62	$ 536.00	$ 12,939.72	$ 156,714.34
58	$ 156,714.34	$ 537.00	$ 14,152.62	$ 171,403.96
59	$ 171,403.96	$ 538.00	$ 15,474.78	$ 187,416.74
60	$ 187,416.74	$ 539.00	$ 16,916.02	$ 204,871.75
61	$ 204,871.75	$ 540.00	$ 18,487.06	$ 223,898.81
62	$ 223,898.81	$ 541.00	$ 20,199.58	$ 244,639.39
63	$ 244,639.39	$ 542.00	$ 22,066.33	$ 267,247.72
64	$ 267,247.72	$ 543.00	$ 24,101.16	$ 291,891.89
65	$ 291,891.89	$ 544.00	$ 26,319.23	$ 318,755.11

Do you honestly think that if the cashier said to David: "You know, sir, for a little extra $318,755, I could add chocolate, whipped cream, colored sugar, and the little cinnamon stick that David would say yes? I don't think anybody likes whip cream that much.

If you've kept from this example that coffee is too expensive at Starbucks, that there are too many calories in the Double Double Mocha Latte, or that if you don't drink coffee at all, you'll be rich, you've missed the point. **A little goes a long way"** means that no matter where your savings come from or their size, even the tiniest amount will make a big difference in the end when you have time on your side.

RULE OF 72

I'm sharing a small, easy, but exciting mathematical rule for estimating the impact of time or level of returns on your capital accumulation.

$$\frac{72}{\text{RETURNS \%}} = \text{NUMBER OF YEARS REQUIRED TO DOUBLE YOUR PORTFOLIO}$$

You also understand that we can also modify this formula to obtain the following:

$$\frac{72}{\text{NBR OF YEARS}} = \text{REQUIRED RETURN \% TO DOUBLE YOUR PORTFOLIO}$$

OK, I open a parenthesis here for all the smart asses of this world who are saying that my formula does not work because it is not true that if I make 72% in one year, my portfolio doubles. To this statement, I answer this: You are absolutely right: the formula only works for yields of less than 20% annually, which is the reality for most people. That said, if you have long-term average annual returns of 72%, give me a call; you just became my new best friend. End of parenthesis.

So to illustrate the concept, if you make a return of 6% per year, your portfolio will double every 12 years (72 / 6 = 12). If you make a return of 8% per year, you will double your portfolio every 9 years (72 / 8 = 9). This means that if you have a portfolio of $100,000 and a 36-year horizon, at 6% per year, your portfolio will double 3X. Your portfolio will go from $100,000 to $200,000 then from $200,000 to $400,000 and finally from $400,000 to $800,000.

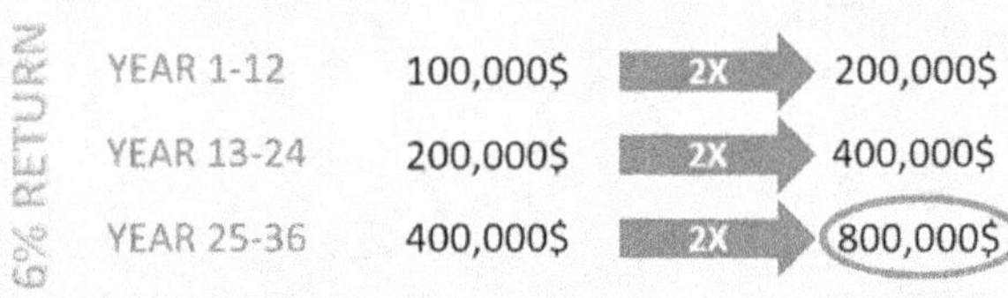

It goes without saying that if you have an average return of 8%, your portfolio will double once again and be worth $1,600,000 ($800,000 X 2) at the end of the same period.

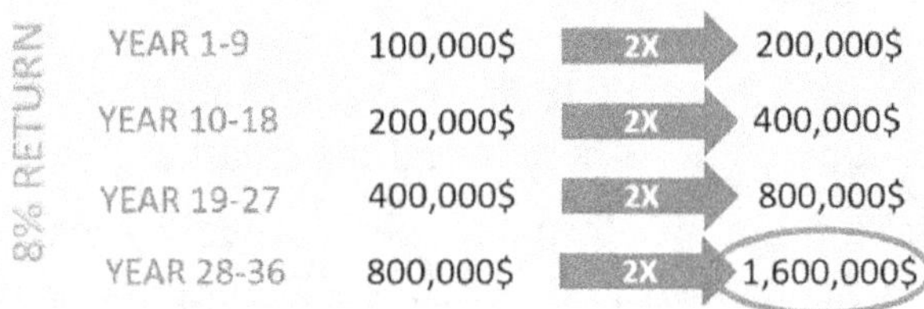

It's incredible what a meager 2% more per year can do, isn't it?

I often meet discouraged people because they are 10 years away from retirement and have accumulated $500,000 for their retirement when their goal was to save $1,000,000. Generally, these same people tell me that they don't see how they will manage to get $500,000 in 10 years if it took them 35 years to save that much. Thirty-five years ago, your portfolio generated very little compounded interest, whereas it is quite different today. If I use my little formula here and my goal is to double my portfolio in 10 years, then you need to achieve an average annual return of 7.2% (72 / 10 years = 7.2%) to reach your goal, assuming that you stop saving. The game is far from lost. <u>Never underestimate the power of compound interest.</u>

OK, IF YOU'RE STILL HERE, CONGRATULATIONS! YOU JUST GOT through the most mathematical chapter of the book. I promise you, I'm locking up the geek in me and keeping the math to a minimum until the end of the book.

PENSION PONZI / LEARNING TO BECOME SELFISH

The government takes what it wants out of your paycheck, then it's power bill, rent, car, groceries, cable, etc. And after all that, it's finally your turn... Assuming there's any left, of course.

Is it just me, or is there something wrong with this picture? I'm not sure, but it seems to me that considering it's your paycheck that you've worked so hard to earn it, maybe you shouldn't be entirely at the bottom of the food chain. Don't tell my kids as I keep telling them to share and think of others, but in this specific case, it's time for you to learn to be selfish because honestly, if you don't, I'm not sure anyone else will do it for you.

I love David Chilton, the author of the book Wealthy Barber. David has his own entertaining and straightforward way of explaining things. If you had to remember only one concept from

The Wealthy Barber (and it would be a shame to remember only one), it would be to learn to pay yourself first.

Saving money is a bit like losing weight. You can have a great plan and the best motivation in the world, but rarely do you have the discipline necessary to achieve your goals. No, but seriously, is there anything more boring than putting money in the bank, paying your debts, or building a nice RSP?

LET'S SEE:

OPTION #1: AN ALL-INCLUSIVE WEEK AT CLUB MED IN THE middle of winter while his colleagues are freezing their asses at -35 degrees.

OPTION #2: PURCHASE A 5-YEAR GIC TO PUT IN THE RSP

Maybe with a bit of marketing, I could change that.

LET'S TRY:

Option #2(A): Purchase a fantastic investment that will ultimately allow you to retire faster and ensure your financial independence for the rest of your life...

No matter how I dress it up, warm sandy beaches, sunshine, tranquility, and margaritas will always have the upper hand over an investment. That's why ultimately, you can't trust yourself when it comes time to do the right thing (that last sentence is probably the strangest thing I've written in this book, I agree, but it's no less true nonetheless). The solution is to take yourself out of the equation, avoid making the decision, and pay yourself first. It's simple: set up a direct debit directly from your bank account for the amount you want to save each paycheck. That money will come out of your account as quickly as possible, will never be in your hands, and will not lead you into temptation. Amen. Too complicated? Open a second bank account and ask your employer to put a portion of your salary into it every paycheck (yes, they can do that). You won't even be aware of it.

. . .

THE REALITY IS THAT INVESTING MONEY IS BORING. AND THAT IF it wasn't necessary, no one would do it. Boring or not, investing for the future is a necessary evil. I want to warn you right away that if you're the kind of optimist who thinks that the government will provide for them, you won't like the next section.

Popularized in 1920 by a certain Charles Ponzi and more recently by a certain Bernard Madoff, a Ponzi scheme basically involves attracting investors by promising them returns that are ultimately paid directly from the funds of more and more new investors. A Ponzi scheme is vulnerable to two events: a stock market crash and, above all, the absence of new investors. It is usually during a market crash when few people are interested in investing that Ponzi schemes are exposed.

MANY PEOPLE MISTAKENLY believe that the Old Age Security pension paid by the federal government results from their accumulated money over their lifetime. This could not be further from the truth. In reality, the pension paid to retirees is paid out of money collected from the income of current workers.

• • •

IN SHORT, THE FEDERAL PENSION IS NOTHING MORE OR LESS THAN a giant Ponzi scheme. It is legal, perhaps, but built on the same foundation, which makes it vulnerable, like other Ponzi schemes, to poor returns but especially to the loss of new contributors.

IN 1952, THE PENSION PAID $480 per year when it was established. You were eligible at age 70, but your life expectancy was 68. Better yet, there were 18 workers to fund each retiree's pension. The total

1952
AVG SALARY = 2,647$ / YR
ANNUAL PENSION = 480$ / YR
ELIGIBILITY = 70 YEARS
LIFE EXPECTANCY = 68 YEARS
BIRTH RATE = 3.6 / WOMEN
WORKER / RETIREE RATIO = 18/1
PENSION FUND TOTAL COST = 148,236,000$

bill for the federal pension program was 148 million.

2022
AVG SALARY = 54,720$ / YR
ANNUAL PENSION = 7623$ / YR
ELIGIBILITY = 65 YEARS
LIFE EXPECTANCY = 83 YEARS
BIRTH RATE = 1.6 / WOMEN
WORKER / RETIREE RATIO = 3/1
PENSION TOTAL COST = 47,000,000,000$

IN 2022 THE PENSION PAID $7,623 per year. You are eligible at age 65, and life expectancy has increased to 83. In 2022, there were three workers to fund each retiree's pension, while the total bill for the federal pension program has grown to 47 billion dollars, 317X more than in 1952. Are you beginning to understand where I'm going with this? In 70 years, the bill multiplied by 317 times, and the number of payers for that same bill was divided by 6 at the same time. It just doesn't add up.

. . .

ACCORDING TO STATISTICS CANADA, AS EARLY AS 2030, THERE will be only 2 workers left to finance each retiree's pension, and the bill will have more than doubled to nearly $108 billion, or 729X more than the initial budget. In short, the pyramid is about to collapse...

2030

WORKER / RETIREE RATIO

2 / 1

PENSION FUND TOTAL COST

108,000,000,000$

Let's be realistic for a second. If you tell me that I'm going to have to split with 17 other workers a $480 bill a year for each person who lives past 70 and that the vast majority of people will die before age 68, that's a good deal. If you tell me that I have to pay $7,683 a year for each person who lives past 65, that the vast majority of people are going to live past 81, and that I'm going to have to assume this burden out of my own pocket because today there are no longer enough people to share this bill with me. I want to renegotiate as soon as possible.

Yes, but François, the government can't cut the pension! Not only can they, but they have already started to do so. In the 2010 budget, they introduced the tax clawback, which allows the government to reduce your pension and even eliminate it entirely if they deem it necessary. And believe me, this is just the beginning...

Why is this chapter called "Be Selfish"? Because, as I mentioned at the beginning if you don't think about yourself, no one else will. Be selfish, and you will have your financial health in your own hands. Hey! I'm not in on gods' secret, and maybe the pension plan is ultimately here to stay. So much the better if I'm wrong; it will be the icing on the cake for you. Regardless, you cannot put yourself at risk by only relying on this amount. Use time (the latte effect) and take control of your financial health. That's the best advice I can give you.

HOW MUCH DOES IT COST? / NEWS FLASH: BANKS ARE NOT NON-PROFIT ORGANIZATIONS

Maybe you can help me. I have worked in finance for 20 years now. I have over one hundred clients. I've asked them all how much I cost them, and only a minority of them have been able to answer me. I've met over one hundred prospects who asked me many questions about my process, my returns, my team, and my experience, but almost none of them asked me how much my services cost. Even worse, many people get uncomfortable when I bring up the subject as if I'm asking them super personal questions about their sex life. **I DON'T GET IT**.

This is Pierre-Jean Jacques, Pierre-Jean Jacques is in mourning. His lawnmower, Lola, with whom he spent every Sunday afternoon for the last 8 years, has just passed. Rest her soul... Pierre-Jean-Jacques must get over this, and although he feels unfaithful to Lola, his lawn is now grown to an alarming length. This is when the process begins. Pierre-Jean-Jacques picks up the 2022 mower guide of the year, surfs the web for the best recommendations, and goes around to all the stores in the area looking for the best mower and, most importantly, the best price. It doesn't matter if he spends $50 of gas to save $15; it's important... Pierre-Jean-Jacques also has an investment advisor who costs him ... no idea, but it's not that important. You're right Pierre Jean Jacques. After all, it only represents hundreds of thousands of dollars...

Although it sounds totally far-fetched, my example is unfortunately not far from reality. The truth is that you probably have no idea how much your investment advisor is really costing you. And even worse, <u>how much it will ultimately cost you</u>. Starting off, if you tell me that you don't pay any fees for your investments because you're in mutual funds, I can't help you other than to say: "Yes, of course, because banks and mutual fund companies are all non-profit organizations that have your best interests at heart and <u>only</u> your interests" (P.S.: If you haven't figured it out yet, I was being sarcastic here). Not only are you paying fees for your mutual funds, but you are also most likely paying much more fees than the average investor. Fund companies have become masters in the art of hiding fees. Please don't be naive. If I may give you a piece of advice, if you are offered a free investment product, take a hike. Either your advisor doesn't know what he is talking about or takes you for a fool. You want to be naive in love, not in business.

> *"Bah Franck! So what if my investments cost me 2% per year instead of 1%... It's not the end of the world; it's just 1%."*

First, I know that Mr. Naïve here (fictitious name once again, I'm sure you've guessed it) did not read my chapter 4, which explains the effect of time on your investments, because if Mr. Naïve had read it, he would have understood that in the long term 1% is enormous. Not convinced?

Let me introduce you to Mr. Smart (do I really need to mention again that I am using fictitious names?). Mr. Smart pays 1% per year to his manager, who rewards him well with an excellent average annual return of 10% (before fees). Mr. Naïve pays 2% per year to his advisor, who is just as good and generates equally impressive average annual returns of 10% (before fees). Mr. Smart and Mr. Naïve are both 25 years old and let their portfolio grow for 40 years because these funds are intended for their retirement. Their 2 portfolios are identical in every way and are exposed to the same level of risk. The only difference: is the fees.

To answer Mr. Naïve, who believes that 1% is not the end of the world, well, if for you $968,489.86 is not the end of the world, I really don't understand why you bought this book in the first place. You realize that Mr. Smart and Mr. Naïve both had the same amount of money initially, both had the same discipline, and both assumed the same risk. Under these circumstances, does it seem fair that Mr. Smart accumulated 45% more or, if you prefer, 968,489.86$ more than Mr. Naïve? (3,140,942$ for Mr. Smart versus 2,172,452$ for Mr. Naive)

MR. SMART	9.00%		
AGE	INITIAL VALUE	RETURNS	FINAL VALUE
26	$100,000.00	$9,000.00	$109,000.00
27	$109,000.00	$9,810.00	$118,810.00
28	$118,810.00	$10,692.90	$129,502.90
29	$129,502.90	$11,655.26	$141,158.16
30	$141,158.16	$12,704.23	$153,862.40
31	$153,862.40	$13,847.62	$167,710.01
32	$167,710.01	$15,093.90	$182,803.91
33	$182,803.91	$16,452.35	$199,256.26
34	$199,256.26	$17,933.06	$217,189.33
35	$217,189.33	$19,547.04	$236,736.37
36	$236,736.37	$21,306.27	$258,042.64
37	$258,042.64	$23,223.84	$281,266.48
38	$281,266.48	$25,313.98	$306,580.46
39	$306,580.46	$27,592.24	$334,172.70
40	$334,172.70	$30,075.54	$364,248.25
41	$364,248.25	$32,782.34	$397,030.59
42	$397,030.59	$35,732.75	$432,763.34
43	$432,763.34	$38,948.70	$471,712.04
44	$471,712.04	$42,454.08	$514,166.13
45	$514,166.13	$46,274.95	$560,441.08
46	$560,441.08	$50,439.70	$610,880.77
47	$610,880.77	$54,979.27	$665,860.04
48	$665,860.04	$59,927.40	$725,787.45
49	$725,787.45	$65,320.87	$791,108.32
50	$791,108.32	$71,199.75	$862,308.07
51	$862,308.07	$77,607.73	$939,915.79
52	$939,915.79	$84,592.42	$1,024,508.21
53	$1,024,508.21	$92,205.74	$1,116,713.95
54	$1,116,713.95	$100,504.26	$1,217,218.21
55	$1,217,218.21	$109,549.64	$1,326,767.85
56	$1,326,767.85	$119,409.11	$1,446,176.95
57	$1,446,176.95	$130,155.93	$1,576,332.88
58	$1,576,332.88	$141,869.96	$1,718,202.84
59	$1,718,202.84	$154,638.26	$1,872,841.09
60	$1,872,841.09	$168,555.70	$2,041,396.79
61	$2,041,396.79	$183,725.71	$2,225,122.50
62	$2,225,122.50	$200,261.03	$2,425,383.53
63	$2,425,383.53	$218,284.52	$2,643,668.05
64	$2,643,668.05	$237,930.12	$2,881,598.17
65	$2,881,598.17	$259,343.84	$3,140,942.01

MR. NAÏF	8.00%		
AGE	INITIAL VALUE	RETURNS	FINAL VALUE
26	$100,000.00	$8,000.00	$108,000.00
27	$108,000.00	$8,640.00	$116,640.00
28	$116,640.00	$9,331.20	$125,971.20
29	$125,971.20	$10,077.70	$136,048.90
30	$136,048.90	$10,883.91	$146,932.81
31	$146,932.81	$11,754.62	$158,687.43
32	$158,687.43	$12,694.99	$171,382.43
33	$171,382.43	$13,710.59	$185,093.02
34	$185,093.02	$14,807.44	$199,900.46
35	$199,900.46	$15,992.04	$215,892.50
36	$215,892.50	$17,271.40	$233,163.90
37	$233,163.90	$18,653.11	$251,817.01
38	$251,817.01	$20,145.36	$271,962.37
39	$271,962.37	$21,756.99	$293,719.36
40	$293,719.36	$23,497.55	$317,216.91
41	$317,216.91	$25,377.35	$342,594.26
42	$342,594.26	$27,407.54	$370,001.81
43	$370,001.81	$29,600.14	$399,601.95
44	$399,601.95	$31,968.16	$431,570.11
45	$431,570.11	$34,525.61	$466,095.71
46	$466,095.71	$37,287.66	$503,383.37
47	$503,383.37	$40,270.67	$543,654.04
48	$543,654.04	$43,492.32	$587,146.36
49	$587,146.36	$46,971.71	$634,118.07
50	$634,118.07	$50,729.45	$684,847.52
51	$684,847.52	$54,787.80	$739,635.32
52	$739,635.32	$59,170.83	$798,806.15
53	$798,806.15	$63,904.49	$862,710.64
54	$862,710.64	$69,016.85	$931,727.49
55	$931,727.49	$74,538.20	$1,006,265.69
56	$1,006,265.69	$80,501.26	$1,086,766.94
57	$1,086,766.94	$86,941.36	$1,173,708.30
58	$1,173,708.30	$93,896.66	$1,267,604.96
59	$1,267,604.96	$101,408.40	$1,369,013.36
60	$1,369,013.36	$109,521.07	$1,478,534.43
61	$1,478,534.43	$118,282.75	$1,596,817.18
62	$1,596,817.18	$127,745.37	$1,724,562.56
63	$1,724,562.56	$137,965.00	$1,862,527.56
64	$1,862,527.56	$149,002.21	$2,011,529.77
65	$2,011,529.77	$160,922.38	$2,172,452.15

-$968,489.86

Even worse, imagine if Mr. Smart and Mr. Naïve continued on the same path in their retirement and both lived to be just 90 years old.

Mr. Smart will have $319,768 per year to enjoy life, while Mr. Naïve will only have $203,513. At the time of his death, Mr. Naïve will have $2,906,372 left on the table. Almost 3 million dollars and all this for a miserable little 1%. **That's what 1% means, Mr. Naïve.**

MR. SMART — 9.00%

AGE	INITIAL VALUE	RETURNS	WITHDRAW	FINAL VALUE
66	$3,140,942.01	$282,684.78	-$319,767.53	$3,103,859.26
67	$3,103,859.26	$279,347.33	-$319,767.53	$3,063,439.07
68	$3,063,439.07	$275,709.52	-$319,767.53	$3,019,381.05
69	$3,019,381.05	$271,744.29	-$319,767.53	$2,971,357.82
70	$2,971,357.82	$267,422.20	-$319,767.53	$2,919,012.49
71	$2,919,012.49	$262,711.12	-$319,767.53	$2,861,956.09
72	$2,861,956.09	$257,576.05	-$319,767.53	$2,799,764.61
73	$2,799,764.61	$251,978.81	-$319,767.53	$2,731,975.89
74	$2,731,975.89	$245,877.83	-$319,767.53	$2,658,086.19
75	$2,658,086.19	$239,227.76	-$319,767.53	$2,577,546.42
76	$2,577,546.42	$231,979.18	-$319,767.53	$2,489,758.07
77	$2,489,758.07	$224,078.23	-$319,767.53	$2,394,068.77
78	$2,394,068.77	$215,466.19	-$319,767.53	$2,289,767.43
79	$2,289,767.43	$206,079.07	-$319,767.53	$2,176,078.97
80	$2,176,078.97	$195,847.11	-$319,767.53	$2,052,158.55
81	$2,052,158.55	$184,694.27	-$319,767.53	$1,917,085.29
82	$1,917,085.29	$172,537.68	-$319,767.53	$1,769,855.43
83	$1,769,855.43	$159,286.99	-$319,767.53	$1,609,374.89
84	$1,609,374.89	$144,843.74	-$319,767.53	$1,434,451.10
85	$1,434,451.10	$129,100.60	-$319,767.53	$1,243,784.17
86	$1,243,784.17	$111,940.58	-$319,767.53	$1,035,957.22
87	$1,035,957.22	$93,236.15	-$319,767.53	$809,425.84
88	$809,425.84	$72,848.33	-$319,767.53	$562,506.64
89	$562,506.64	$50,625.60	-$319,767.53	$293,364.71
90	$293,364.71	$26,402.82	-$319,767.53	$0.00

$7,994,188.23

MR. NAÏF — 8.00%

AGE	INITIAL VALUE	RETURNS	WITHDRAW	FINAL VALUE
66	$2,172,452.15	$173,796.17	-$203,512.66	$2,142,735.66
67	$2,142,735.66	$171,418.85	-$203,512.66	$2,110,641.84
68	$2,110,641.84	$168,851.35	-$203,512.66	$2,075,980.53
69	$2,075,980.53	$166,078.44	-$203,512.66	$2,038,546.30
70	$2,038,546.30	$163,083.70	-$203,512.66	$1,998,117.34
71	$1,998,117.34	$159,849.39	-$203,512.66	$1,954,454.07
72	$1,954,454.07	$156,356.33	-$203,512.66	$1,907,297.73
73	$1,907,297.73	$152,583.82	-$203,512.66	$1,856,368.88
74	$1,856,368.88	$148,509.51	-$203,512.66	$1,801,365.73
75	$1,801,365.73	$144,109.26	-$203,512.66	$1,741,962.32
76	$1,741,962.32	$139,356.99	-$203,512.66	$1,677,806.64
77	$1,677,806.64	$134,224.53	-$203,512.66	$1,608,518.51
78	$1,608,518.51	$128,681.48	-$203,512.66	$1,533,687.32
79	$1,533,687.32	$122,694.99	-$203,512.66	$1,452,869.64
80	$1,452,869.64	$116,229.57	-$203,512.66	$1,365,586.55
81	$1,365,586.55	$109,246.92	-$203,512.66	$1,271,320.81
82	$1,271,320.81	$101,705.66	-$203,512.66	$1,169,513.81
83	$1,169,513.81	$93,561.10	-$203,512.66	$1,059,562.25
84	$1,059,562.25	$84,764.98	-$203,512.66	$940,814.56
85	$940,814.56	$75,265.16	-$203,512.66	$812,567.06
86	$812,567.06	$65,005.36	-$203,512.66	$674,059.76
87	$674,059.76	$53,924.78	-$203,512.66	$524,471.88
88	$524,471.88	$41,957.75	-$203,512.66	$362,916.96
89	$362,916.96	$29,033.36	-$203,512.66	$188,437.65
90	$188,437.65	$15,075.01	-$203,512.66	$0.00

$5,087,816.62

-$2,906,371.60

A gap of 1% may seem huge to you, but it is not uncommon to see this kind of gap. I have even seen discrepancies of 2%. In the previous example, even a 0.1% spread would have cost $350,000. I don't know about you, but I'm not the type to leave $350,000 on the table.

I know what you are thinking right now; how awesome would it be if you didn't have to pay any fees at all. My answer to those wishful thinkers is "You could also save money by being your own dentist."

Your financial advisor is offering you expertise, and yes, in return, he expects to be paid (remember, nothing is free). Several studies have been conducted on this subject. The Inter-university Research Center for Organizational Analysis (CIRANO) has shown that when comparing two identical investors, those who have benefited from an advisor's financial expertise for four to six years have 58% more financial assets than individuals who did not have an advisor. Morningstar estimates the added value of having an investment advisor at 1.82% per year (after fees).

Remember the example of Mr. Smart and Mr. Naive, where 1% represents an added value of +$2,906,372? Well +1.82% per year represent an extra $6,452,866.

A financial consultant's advice is truly an asset. It's only normal that they would expect to be compensated for their services. Just be cautious that you are not overpaying for the services. You can have a gem of a paperboy; it doesn't mean you'd want to pay him 250K a year.

The point I'm trying to make is that we all have a little Pierre-Jean-Jacques in us. We should let him work as hard when it comes to shopping for investments as we do when shopping for a new lawnmower.

Do you want to be Mr. Smart or Mr. Naive? The ball is in your court.

RISK 101 / JUMPING
FROM A PLANE
WITHOUT A PARACHUTE

What is riskier: jumping out of an airplane with a parachute or without a parachute? If you answered without a parachute, then congratulations, you are part of the 95% of our society that does not have the correct perception of what risk is, at least from a financial point of view.

In investing, the risk is UNCERTAINTY. Too often, the probability of getting hurt, injured, or even killed is mixed with the term risk, whereas in investment, it is not. Investors do not like uncertainty. The more uncertainty there is in a market, the more volatile and riskier it becomes. Therefore, from a financial point of view, it is much riskier to jump out of a plane with a parachute than without one because the person who jumps without a parachute faces little uncertainty (death is inevitable), whereas the person who jumps with a parachute is probably wondering if his parachute will open or not.

Not convinced, hear me out: Let's go back to 2008. The financial crisis is in full swing, the U.S. banking system is on the verge of collapse, the Dow Jones just dropped 41% in the last 6 months. The U.S. government announced a first intervention to follow somewhere in the next 6 months. 30 days later, the Dow rebounded by 15%. Heeelllllooo! The government hasn't injected a single penny yet. It's all about uncertainty. Most recently, you heard the news that England voted in favoring Brexit, and it's the end of the world as we know it. The market instantly drops over 10%. Two weeks later, the markets went up 12%. The vote was not overturned; the Brexit is still well and truly official. Is it just me or...

INVESTORS HATE SURPRISES.

That's nice, Franck, so how about you tell me how to measure uncertainty?

Uncertainty can't be measured, but it is possible to measure how investments react to surprise. This measure is called standard deviation. Standard deviation, which I will exempt you from calculating, is a measure of volatility. The higher the standard deviation, the higher your portfolio's volatility, and vice versa. You want to have an idea of the level of risk of your portfolio. Your portfolio will (in 95% of the cases) have returns that will fluctuate within + or - 2 times your standard deviation compared to its average return. For example, you have a portfolio with an average return of 7% with a standard deviation of 5%, then 95% of the time, your return will be between **-3%** (7%- (2*5%)) and **+17%** (7% + (2*5%)).

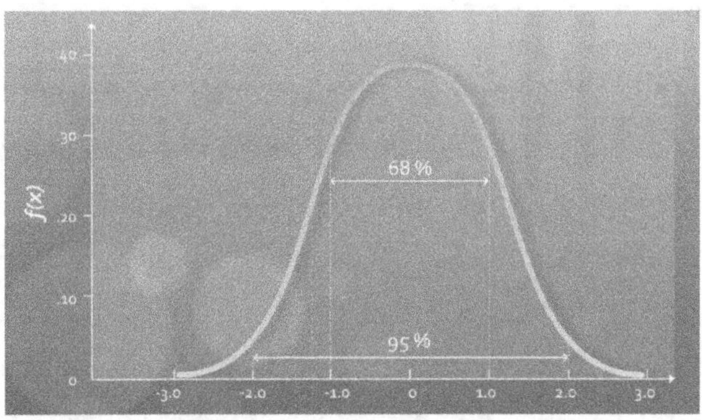

I promised you at the beginning of this book that I wasn't going to make you nauseous, and for that reason, I'm going to stop the math here. What I really want you to remember here is that yield alone means absolutely nothing.

For example, Both Nicolas and Justine's investment advisors generated a 10% return last year. Who has the better advisor?

The answer: **not a clue.**

• • •

WHY? BECAUSE WE ARE MISSING THE ESSENTIAL INFORMATION TO find out: the risk. If I tell you now that Nicolas' portfolio has a standard deviation of 25% and Justine's has a standard deviation of 5%, who has the better advisor?

Considering that Nicolas' advisor risked 25% of the account to generate a 10% return, while Justine's advisor risked only 5% to generate the same return, it is clear that Justine's advisor is way more efficient. What would happen now if Nicolas' advisor had, with his current level of risk, obtained a return of 20%? Same conclusion.

WAIT A MINUTE, François! Are you really telling me that the advisor who makes 10% is better than the one who makes 20%? Yes, that's precisely what I'm telling you. Your advisor's job is to ensure that the risk you take is adequately compensated. Suppose your advisor generates $2 of profit for every $1 you risk (10% return / 5% standard deviation) like Justine's. In that case, you are in a much better company than if your advisor generates $0.80 of profit for every $1 of risk (20% return / 25% standard deviation).

Imagine walking into a casino, and there are two blackjack tables in front of you. For a $100 bet at table # 1, the dealer will give you an $80 profit for each winning hand. At table # 2, for the same $100 bet, each winning hand will earn you a $200 profit. If you choose to sit at table #1, either you don't understand the concept (or have a severe gambling problem).

As I said earlier, and I'll say it again because it's not just crucial; its, in fact, one of the most essential points in this book. Your advisor's job is to maximize your portfolio returns based on <u>your</u> level of risk. It's not to maximize your return regardless of risk nor convince you to take more risks. Remember my risk/return ratio?

$$\frac{\text{RETURN \%}}{\text{RISK \%}} = \text{THE HIGHER THIS RATIO IS, THE BETTER IS YOUR ADVISOR}$$

This is the only way to compare apples to apples when analyzing your advisor's work quality. Your advisor has three options to improve his ratio: increase his return (without significantly increasing his risk), decrease his risk (without significantly decreasing his return), or, in the best of all possible worlds, increase his return by decreasing his risk (easier said than done, but still doable). One thing your advisor should never, oh never, do is try to get you to take more risks than you are actually comfortable with. Their job is to properly determine your risk tolerance level, give you the best results within your investor profile and manage your expectations.

THE WORST THREE THINGS AN ADVISOR CAN DO ARE:

STRIKE ONE

Your advisor is not aware of your accurate risk tolerance level. He manages as he sees fit according to his comfort level. It's only a matter of time before your portfolio drops more than you can handle, and you pull the plug at the worst possible time when everything is cheap.

STRIKE TWO

Your advisor is aware of your risk tolerance but chooses to ignore it, thinking that their job is to get you the highest possible return no matter what. You will one day lose more money than you think was even possible, and you won't understand why.

STRIKE THREE

With the best intentions in the world, your advisor creates a portfolio in line with your risk tolerance but neglects to rebalance your portfolio or update your profile as the years go by.

RISK TOLERANCE IS A VERY PERSONAL THING; IT IS NOT TRUE that because you are 18 years old, you can assume more risk or, conversely, that because you are 88 years old, you cannot assume any risk at all. Each individual is unique; your life experiences, personality, background, and education are all factors that will ultimately influence your investment profile. The most important thing here is to have a tailored portfolio that will allow you to stay the course in good and bad markets. At the beginning of this book, I talked about it: "Emotion = Cancer" when talking about investing. You're bound to slip up if your portfolio takes you out of your comfort zone and makes you emotional. Whether you are responsible for your own management or have an investment advisor, you should always be comfortable with the risk level of your portfolio.

ACTIVE AND PASSIVE MANAGEMENT / TRYING TO BE RIGHT OR TRYING NOT TO BE WRONG

In my opinion, there are two kinds of investors, those who try to be right and those who try not to be wrong. You might think they are the same thing, but it couldn't be further from the truth. The investor trying to be right wants to create alpha (in short, they want to make a difference), while the one trying not to be wrong is satisfied with the result. There is a reason why index investing has enjoyed such a resurgence in popularity for several years. Creating alpha is not easy. It requires expertise, hard work, and discipline. In short, it's not for everyone. If you tell me that you want to manage your own investments, have neither the knowledge, nor the time, nor the interest, are ready to live with the whims of the market: "Be my guest" and go buy an exchange-traded fund (ETF). This type of product is just right for you. With that being said, if you are an industry professional, a mutual fund company, or a hedge fund that is paid handsomely by its clients because you generate alpha for them and buy them a stock index (ETF), I honestly don't know how you sleep at night.

The reality is that active management is a dying art, so much so that many industry players have simply stopped trying. I could easily pull up a list of mutual funds that charge you 1.5% or even 2.0% to generate alpha but only hold one position: the same stock index they are supposed to beat (that you could easily buy by yourself for less than 0.25% by the way). You will agree that their chances of success are rather slim, especially when you consider their fees. I have often questioned investment advisors who only do index investing. They have proudly explained that their strategy is more brilliant because next time the market falls, they will have a good excuse to explain their losses. TRYING NOT TO BE WRONG.

Is it laziness? Are investors capitulated and adopting an "IF YOU CANT BEAT THEM, JOIN THEM" attitude? I don't know but what I do know is :

1. That you're never going to stand out from the crowd by doing what the rest of the pack does.
2. That if you want to make money, you have to be proactive. Losing money should never be acceptable.

As Warren Buffett (yes, him again) said it so well, there are two rules in investing:

1. Never lose money
2. Never forget rule no.1

Don't get me wrong, I'm not telling you that you will never lose money in the stock market. The stock market goes through cycles of growth and decline; it's a known fact. What I'm saying is that accepting that you're going to lose money because that's the reality of the market instead of struggling and trying to profit from the situation would be inappropriate.

Yes, but François, what exactly is active management? Active management is like doing a fantasy hockey pool with your friends. Your job is to choose the best players and leave the worst to the others. The success of your hockey pool relies heavily on your ability to pick players who will outperform expectations while avoiding every Scott Gomez in the league. In short, to manage actively is to expose oneself; it is to go to the bat, to put one's head on the block. Basically, it's risking looking like a fool. No wonder fewer and fewer people are doing it. Now imagine that I offered you, at the very beginning of the pool, the option of choosing all the players in the league with the certainty that in no case you will win your pool but also that in no case you will end last. Would you take it? In other words, do you play to win (active management) or simply not to lose (passive)?

Active management, you guessed it, also implies that you are active. No, I'm not talking about day trading here, but neither am I buying a stock and holding it for the next 50 years. The days of the untouchables, the "too big to fail," are over. You want to make me lose it completely, try to justify why you have 70% of your account in only 1 stock under the pretext that it is untouchable.

. . .

To all those eternal romantic optimists, I say this: Nortel Network, Enron, Leeman Brothers, Air Canada, General Motors, WorldCom. Not convinced? SwissAir, Kmart, Washington Mutual, C.I.T. Group, Conseco, Chrysler, Texaco, Lyondell, United Airline, Delta Airline, Pacific Gas, CanWest, Quebecor World, Sears, Target, Toys R U.S., and I could go on and on. Did you know that over 83 countries have gone bankrupt in the last 200 years*? And not just any country! Germany twice, Japan, England (4 times), and yes, even the United States 5 times rather than one (the last time in 1933). Is there anyone who still wants to talk about untouchables? No, there are no more untouchables which means that you can't buy a quality title and just forget about it. Connor McDavid might be the player that wins your fantasy pool this year. I'm not convinced he'll win your pool 20 years from now.

For over 20 years now, I have driven to the office every morning and evening from Monday to Friday, which is 60 minutes of traffic on a good day, and I can proudly say I've never had an accident. At 60 minutes a day X 250 days a year X 20 years, that's 300,000 minutes of accident-free driving. My trick? I am attentive to the road, to my environment, aware of the risks and dangers, and remain on the lookout. Portfolio management is precisely the same thing. I mentioned it before, and I will mention it again. Your job as an active portfolio manager is not to predict the future but to react and adjust to the many caprices of the markets. Choosing what to buy is not even half the battle here, just like getting behind the wheel of my car. Knowing what to do with it once you've made up your mind is the real battle. I won't lie to you, this is a lot of work, and it's definitely a lot more stressful than simply buying something and forgetting about it for the next 50 years. I could settle for taking the bus or the subway every morning and save myself the stress and trouble. Still, I have to admit that some definite advantages are linked to the alternative. Again, it's a matter of taste, and it's not for everyone. But you should know that active management is in no way more dangerous than passive management. In fact, I would say that it is less dangerous. I personally would much rather be in control than a passenger. Anyone who, like me, has ever been stuck in a subway train for many painful hours understands the analogy.

Want to stand out as a portfolio manager? There are no shortcuts. You need to understand what you're buying, know its strengths and weaknesses, and constantly keep your eyes on the road.

REAL ESTATE AS AN INVESTMENT / OK, NOW YOU MAY HATE ME

Here we are at last: the least popular chapter of the book. Why the least popular? Because I'm going to go against popular belief and upset many people. Ultimately, I even expect that many people will choose to ignore the entire chapter because it's just easier to do that than to consider that I might be right.

So there you go:

In most cases, real estate <u>is not</u> an investment, at least not a good one.

That's it. I said it... Now for all those who are still here, here is the explanation.

. . .

THE LAROUSSE DICTIONARY DEFINES INVESTMENT AS AN operation that makes it possible to renew and **increase** your capital. Little Robert, for his part, defines an investment as a decision by which an individual, a company, or a community allocates its own resources or borrowed funds to **increase** its stock of productive assets.

Both definitions agree on one thing, and the keyword here is increase, whereas unfortunately, real estate does not often meet this qualifier in practice.

I can already hear many of you saying: "What are you talking about? My father bought his house in 1950 for 50,000$, and he just sold it for 250,000$. That's 500%! To which I reply: "No, over 70 years, that's 2.33% per year". In fact, if the house does not sell for at least 594,501$, well, I'm sorry to tell you, but your father has lost money while inflation since 1950 was 3.60% per year. If I also consider that the Canadian Real Estate Association estimates that the annual cost of maintaining the house is 2% of the value of the house + an average of 1% in property taxes and that if your father had at any time a mortgage on the residence even at a rate of 2% interest, then your father would have had to sell his house for a minimum of $16,108,599 to even begin to consider it as an investment

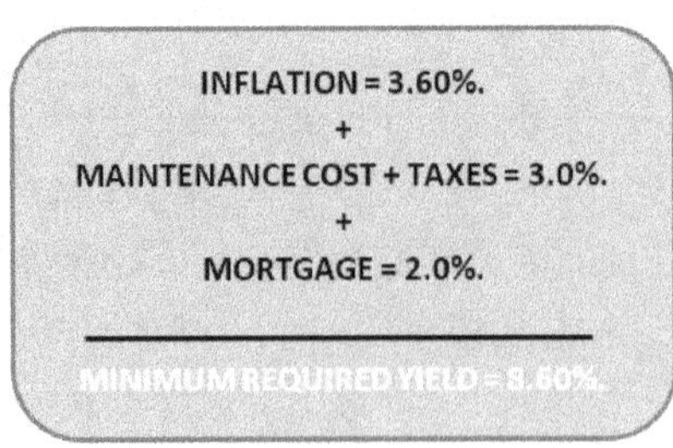

Still not convinced then take a good look at this. According to the latest research*, the returns by asset class from 1950 to 2016 are as follows:

According to this data, your father will have to sell his house for at least 1.857 million dollars to obtain the same return as a simple treasury bond, 3.8 million to obtain a return equivalent to that of the 5-year G.I.C.s or 101 million dollars

REAL ESTATE	2.43%
INFLATION	3.60%
T-BILLS	5.30%
G.I.C. 5YRS	6.40%
DEX FIXED INCOME LT	7.60%
CONSERVATIVE PORTFOLIO	8.77%
BALANCED PORTFOLIO	9.50%
TSX	9.80%
GROWTH PORTFOLIO	10.33%
EMERGING MARKET	10.50%
S&P500	11.50%

to obtain a return close to that of the S&P500 (U.S. market index). I hope for him that his house is located on an oil field or a diamond mine ... Otherwise, it's a waste of time.

REAL ESTATE	$268,455.37
INFLATION	$594,501.40
T-BILLS	$1,857,616.19
GIC 5YRS	$3,844,890.37
DEX FIXED INCOME LT	$8,430,027.62
CONSERVATIVE PORTFOLIO	$17,972,521.08
BALANCED PORTFOLIO	$28,705,052.58
TSX	$34,764,325.88
GROWTH PORTFOLIO	$48,699,362.58
EMERGING MARKET	$54,241,222.08
S&P500	$101,908,573.21

I know very well that some of you are telling yourselves that the 2.43% average return since 1950 is not a good indicator. In contrast, the reality of recent years has instead shown a boom and that specific sectors are more awarded than others (Vancouver, Victoria, and Toronto, for example).

TAUX DE RENDEMENT ANNUEL MOYEN DE L'IMMOBILIER CANADIEN PAR RÉGION MÉTROPOLITAINE DE 1980 À 2012	Nominal %	Réel %
CANADA	5.4	2.1
Vancouver	6.4	3.2
Victoria	5.5	3.4
Calgary	4.7	1.2
Edmonton	4.4	1.0
Regina	5.9	2.5
Saskatoon	5.3	2.0
Winnipeg	5.2	1.9
Toronto	6.1	2.7
Ottawa	5.5	2.2
Halifax	5.2	2.0
Saint John	4.1	0.9

Remarque : Le taux de rendement réel de l'immobilier est calculé au moyen de l'IPC d'ensemble pour chaque région métropolitaine.
Sources : L'Association canadienne de l'immeuble, Statistique Canada.

I do admit that the situation has been different lately, but with that being said, *the Canadian Real Estate Association* recently published a study to this effect, which clearly illustrates this famous boom.

I think we can agree that an average annual return of 2.1% is not a very impressive selling point in such a favorable period. Especially not when you consider that it costs an average of 3% per year to maintain the quality and, by the same token, the value of your property or that, in fact, very few people do not have a mortgage. Even if the last three decades offered extraordinary returns, does anyone sincerely believe that real estate can maintain such a trend for another half-century? The Americans tried it, and look how it ended in 2008.

Let's talk about the Americans! If you think it's any different South of the Border, think again. The *National Association of Realtors* of the United States published in 2006 the average return at the national level since 1968 for a house of average size without a mortgage (always without considering the average maintenance costs of 3% per annum). Drum roll.................. 1%

Yes, a meager **1%**. That was in 2006, just <u>before</u> 4 years of consecutive declines (2007-2010) that saw the real estate market lose **-30%** of its value in a few years. In short, we have nothing to envy about our neighbors to the south with our 2.1%.

John D Rockefeller is inevitably the big argument of all the great defenders of real estate. According to the New York Times, John D. Rockefeller's fortune is 340 billion dollars. By comparison, Bill Gates is $89 billion. It is true that Rockefeller's fortune is basically linked to real estate. But the nuance with Mr. and Mrs. everyone who buys a house in the suburbs with the double garage and the swimming pool, Rockefeller, himself, bought land and not just any land. There is a massive difference between buying a house with a mortgage that you live in and therefore maintaining or buying vacant land and paying cash for it. Especially if, ultimately, there is oil below this ground. Real estate may very well indeed be the foundation of the Rockefeller empire, but in the end, it was oil that made its fortune. Real estate, here, was only a medium to achieve its ends.

I could give you as many statistics as you want, but nothing explains better why real estate is not an investment than common sense. Banks use a system called the 5 C's to determine one's solvability:

1. COLLATERAL: The guarantee offered in exchange for the debt (real estate value or any other personal assets)
2. CONDITIONS: Loan characteristics include terms, rates, and how the funds are intended to be used.
3. CAPITAL: The portion of the borrower's own capital invested in the project (Cash Down)

4. CHARACTER: Borrower's credit rating
5. CAPACITY: The ability of the borrower to repay the debt, taking into account his actual level of debt, his income, and the stability of employment

Imagine your distant cousin Gary, whom you haven't seen in 10 years, knocks on your door tonight and asks you to lend him some money to allow him to carry out his latest project: **Pet Rock** selling rocks as an alternative to pets. The fact that your cousin has no income (capacity), offers no guarantees (collateral), that you do not believe in his project (conditions) or that your cousin is ready to risk your capital but only yours (capital), and that he has gone bankrupt three times in the last 10 years (character) are all excellent reasons to close the door in his face. But for a bank, capacity has always been, and always will be, the most important of the five components. Why? Simply because it is the most reliable, plain, and straightforward.

I'm sure some of you have experienced it, as I know many of my clients did. You just retired and realized that now that you have retired, you don't want to shovel snow, mow grass, or spend time taking care of the pool anymore. On top of it, it's getting obvious that the house was way too big now that the kids have left the nest. It's time to enjoy life now, play golf, bridge, learn to tap dance, and travel the world. And a condo seems like the perfect option for all that. OK, maybe your neighbors won't appreciate the tap-dancing much, but you've made up your mind anyways. Since you've read my book, you know that not only debt and leverage are not the devil in person but, more importantly, that real estate, no matter if it's a house or a condo, is a bad investment. So you call your banker to ask for a mortgage for that brand new condo. The banker prepares his file as follows:

- **Collateral** : The condo worth $800,000 — YES

- **Condition** : standard loan 75% of equity — YES

- **Capital** : down payment of $200,000 + 10,000,000$ in assets — YES

- **Character** : impeccable credit record — YES

- **Capacity:** official income of 7000$ / yr — NO

It used to be a formality for you, but your financing is denied for the first time in your life. Why? You don't have enough income anymore. What do you mean by no income? Franck, I have a 10 million dollar portfolio. You generate me a 10% return per year on average, that 1 million per year, enough to pay the whole mortgage every year, for god sake. I understand this, and I agree with you, but that's not how banks see things. You see, that bank has no guarantee that you won't withdraw that 10 million tomorrow and spend it all on bubble gum. I agree it would be a lot of bubble gum, but you understand their concerns. Without capacity, you are not solvable even with all the other ones. Only capacity provides some consistency, making it the most crucial component when a bank analyzes your credit file.

You're probably wondering where I'm going with my 5 C's and how they relate to real estate. Bear with me; I'm getting there.

We've already established that your capacity is the main criterion for borrowing money. I haven't mentioned to you yet that since the increase in average wages historically barely keeps up with inflation, it's unlikely that your capacity will grow faster than inflation. If your capacity is your purchasing power and your purchasing power follows inflation, then real estate prices must also follow inflation closely. That's the law of supply and demand, which explains why the historical rate of return on real estate is below that long-term inflation rate.

It is essential to put a caveat here because we should not get generalized. In certain specific cases, it may be that real estate proves to be an investment and sometimes even a good one. There are sometimes excellent short-term opportunities in a rental property or if you have the talent to flip properties that are in dire need of love. But we shouldn't make the mistake of assuming that these exceptions are the rule. For the average person buying a house to live in with their family, **real estate is most likely not an investment, at the very least, not a good one.**

Finally, I want to be clear here, I am not telling you not to buy a house. Having a home meets many of the basic needs of Maslow's pyramid.

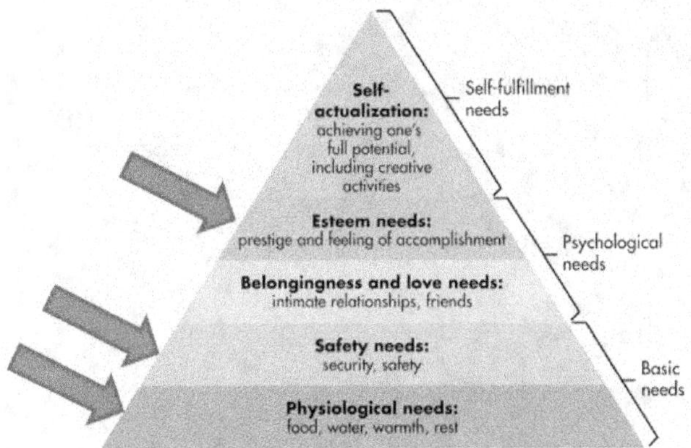

We should simply call an apple an apple and realize that real estate is not an investment but a form of forced saving, which in the end is not a bad thing at all because, let's be honest, without a mortgage, many people would never have saved anything.

P.S.: Pet Rock is an actual company. In 1975, Gary Dahl, an advertising executive from Los Gatos, California, was at a bar one night listening to friends complain about their pets. He joked that he would rather keep a rock as a pet. Then he decided to write an official 32-page training manual and started selling them. They were packaged in boxes with air holes and little straw beds. The craze lasted only six months, but Gary Dahl was $15 million richer by then. The lesson is that sometimes it pays to take jokes seriously. As of 2012, pet rocks were made available again.

P.P.S.: maybe despite all the facts, you should have invested in your cousin Gary's idea after all. (L.O.L.)

IT'S A CRAZY WORLD WE'RE LIVING IN / WHEN NONSENSE ACTUALLY STARTS MAKING SENSE

By definition, the bursting of a financial bubble is characterized by a market decline of 2 times its standard deviation (hey, now you know what a standard deviation is, how convenient). In theory, this kind of behavior should occur once every 44 years. Since 1925, we can count more than 30 financial bubbles, equivalent to a bubble every 3 years. You are free to interpret this information as you please.

- -You can go with the hyper optimistic (aka hyper naive) approach and say that we now have several bubbles in the bank and are now good for 1320 years (44 years X 30 bubbles = 1320 years) of stable growth without any bubbles.

Or

- -You can join me in the category of logical people who have understood that theory is worth what it's worth and that reality is something else entirely.

When a crash occurs, we learn a lot in the short term, a little less in the medium term, and nothing at all in the long term. Why is this? Because memory is a faculty that forgets. It's inevitable; every time the markets go up, investors think it will go up forever. Every time the markets go down, it's a never-ending hole. Ironically, soon after a bubble bursts, it always becomes obvious why the correction happened. Inevitably, comes after the question, "How could we be so naive when the signs were so obvious?" It happened in 2008 and 2000 and in the other previous bubbles. Worse, it will happen again in the next bubbles. Because even if the bursting of a bubble temporarily gives us a certain clarity, this lucidity seems to evaporate with the return of positive yields. In other words, we become too busy making money again to be suspicious of something we all know: the market works in cycles, and everything that goes up eventually comes down. I have always found the theoretical business cycle curve that looks like the letter S sideways very amusing:

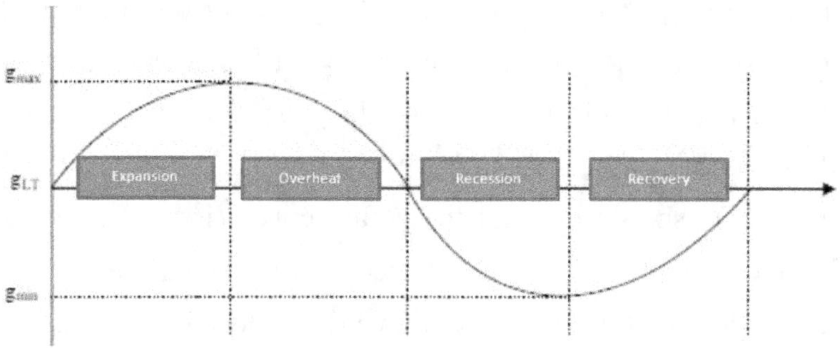

Amusing because I did the exercise to satisfy my curiosity to compare this curve with the curve of the markets over history. I did not manage to find a single period close to that S sideway. Based on your personal experience, do you recall a period where the markets simply and quietly started a slow yet predictable decline after X years of stable growth? No, the market cycle curve looks a lot more like the letter Z sideways. With the Z shape market goes up for a certain time at different pace but usually turns around in a non-stable and non-predictable way.

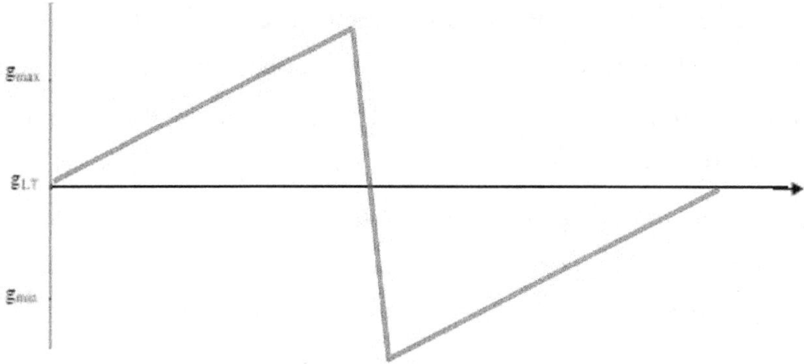

But Things get particularly interesting when you combine the two curves. Do the exercise and draw your S sideway curve on a piece of paper in black and then add your Z sideways curve in red on top of it. The standard S curve (in black) represents what the markets <u>should do</u>, and the actual curve (in red) represents what the markets actually <u>do</u>. It then becomes clear here that the markets do not always do what they are supposed to do (not a big surprise here, I agree);

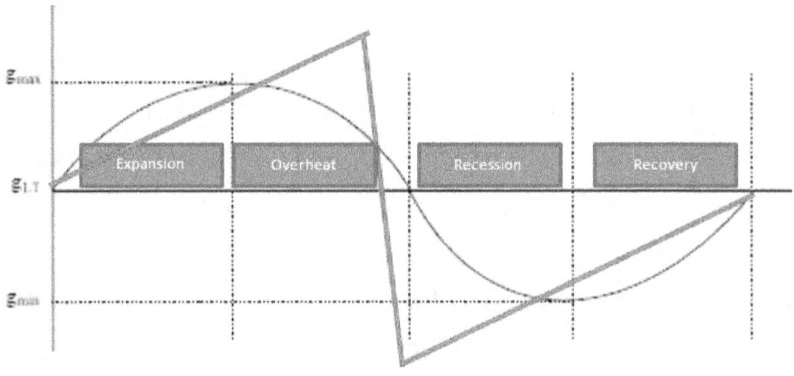

You will notice that although both lines are not identical in any way, they do intersect once in a while. When this happens, you could say that the theoretical market is in line with the actual market. But as you can see, it's not happening very often. If you start at the beginning of the growth phase, when the market starts to climb up to the point where the black line and red line intersect, I would call this phase the justifiable growth phase.

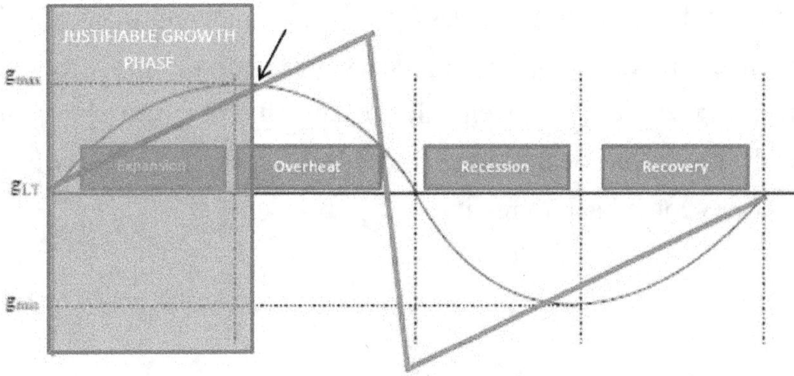

However, from that crossing point to the very end of your red curve ascension, you are in a period of irrational growth. It is during this period that the famous evaporation of clarity that I mentioned earlier occurs. It is during this phase that one becomes so obsessed with making more and more money that one forgets all sense of caution. This is the phase "what goes up, goes up forever," although clearly, at this point, the growth is already no longer justified.

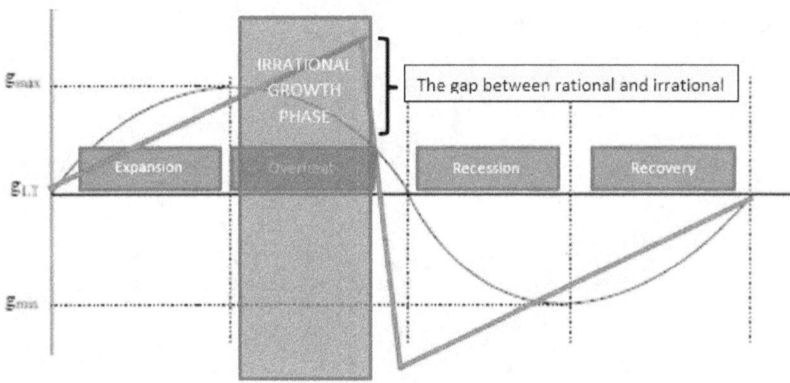

The next phase follows as the markets inevitably eventually change direction and the actual curve (red curve) drops from the very highest level. It eventually reaches the next crossing point with the theoretical curve (the black one). In other words, markets come back to reality.

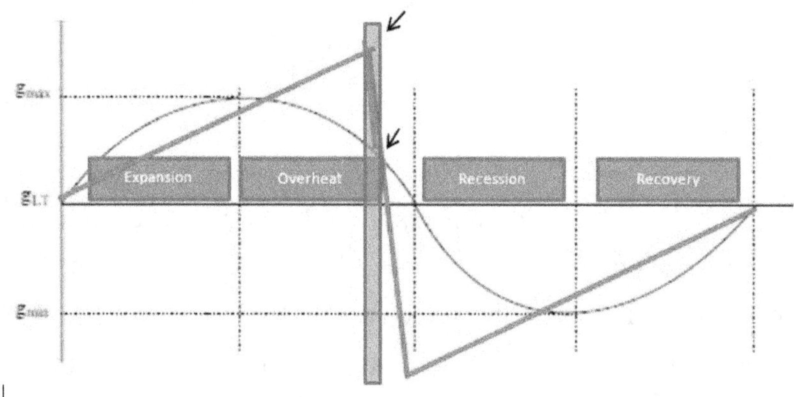

This is followed by the next phase, during which the fall of the markets takes exaggerated proportions. We are in the pessimistic phase of "what goes down, goes down forever," and the market loses way more than justifiable.

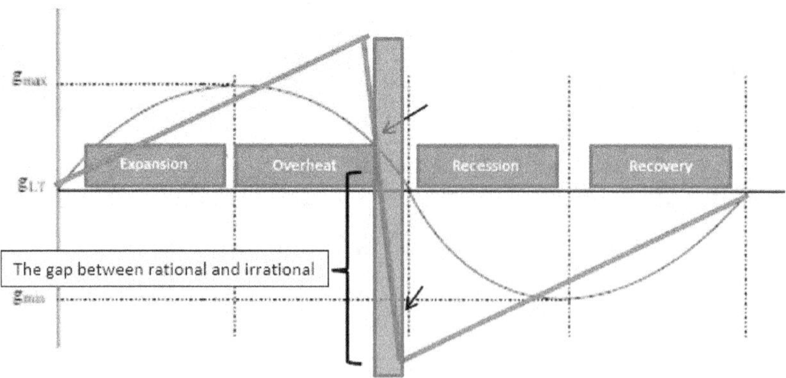

Finally, it is the last phase, the recovery one, as the markets recover and return to more justifiable levels. Before overdoing it again and starting the cycle again and again

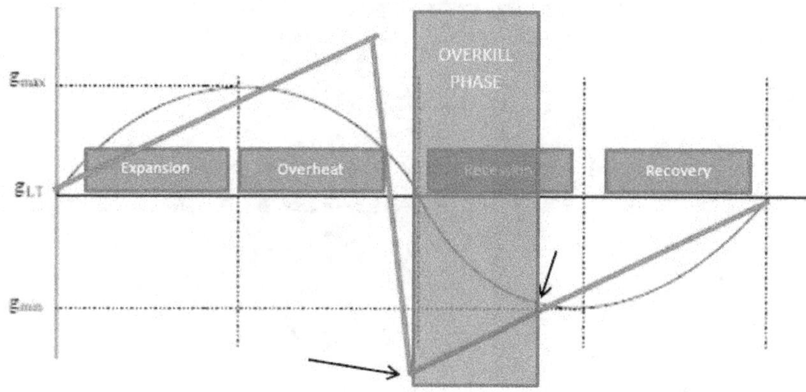

In short, the market suffers from a bipolar schizophrenic personality disorder, while it sometimes behaves rationally (in blue) and at times entirely irrationally (in red).

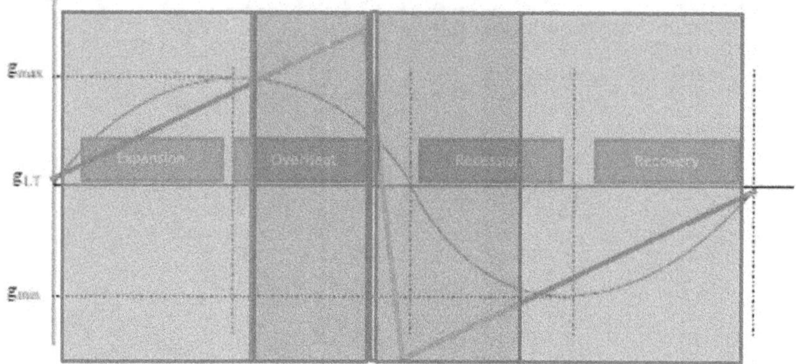

Although this phenomenon has always existed, it is easy to see that in the last 20 years, the phenomenon has been amplified, whereas, in fact, the irrational period in the cycle seems to be shorter from 1940 to 1999 than what we've been witnessing since 2000.

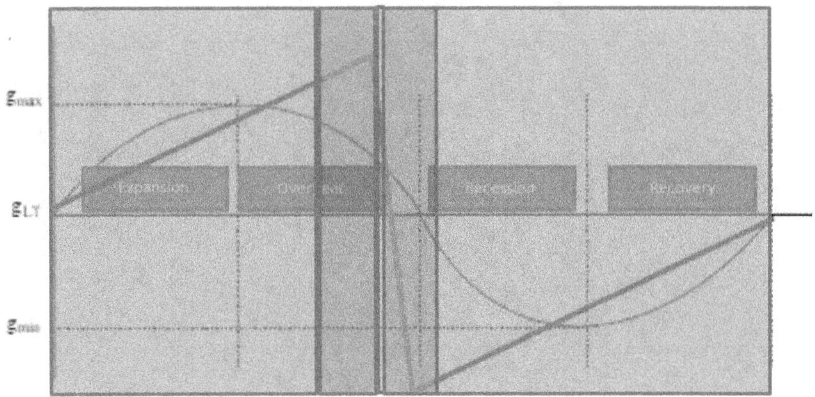

This partly explains why we just had the worst two consecutive cycles in history. -50% for the 2000 cycle followed by -56% in 2007.

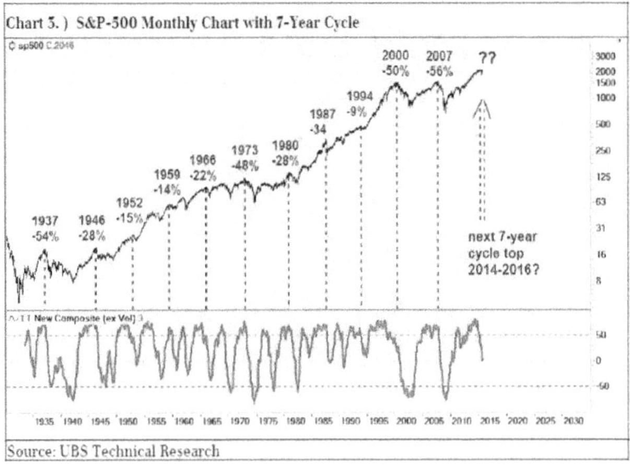

Do these cycles represent a simple misstep or a new reality? Personally, I believe it is the latter. The markets have significantly evolved since the days when there were only a handful of managers (354 licensed brokers in 1864) who placed their trades by hand and followed the good old "Ticker Tape ."In 2022, we are in the age of technology, where information circulates at the speed of light (literally), where anyone can improvise himself as a manager and trade in real-time using his smartphone. We now live in the era of Robo-advisors, artificial intelligence (Watson), and high-frequency trading (H.F.T.). In my humble opinion, it is also these famous T.H.F. who are most to blame for our new reality.

What does a T.H.F. stand for, you wonder? Basically, it's a super-computer that executes financial transactions at high speed (1 microsecond), controlled by computer algorithms that manage so much stock market data that it would be impossible for 100,000 humans to analyze it in real-time. A THF system makes, on average, 800,000 transactions per second, which means, for comparison, that it would take 10 minutes and 20 seconds for a single T.H.F. system to replicate all of the 496 million transactions that took place in all the world markets for the whole of 1950.

In 2000, T.H.F. represented 10% of all equity transactions. In 2009, T.H.F. represented more than 73% of all market transactions*. Coincidence?

When you think of it, it makes perfect sense that markets become more and more irrational if more and more of the market's actions are dictated by machines unable to measure the imponderable. These machines may not have created these irrational periods because they have always been part of the picture. Still, they have certainly helped amplify their effects.

So what does this mean for us, ordinary investors? This means that you have to be extra **careful** when things go too well and **bold when** it seems like the sun will never come out again. It's been a while since we treated ourselves with one of those famous Warren Buffetts quotes, so here is another one:

 "Be fearful when others are greedy, and greedy when others are fearful."

— WARREN BUFFETT

IF GOD HIMSELF WAS A GOOD FACEBOOK FRIEND AND GAVE ME advance notice of the exact moment the markets would turn, my life would be amazing. I would take advantage of every upswing, squeeze the last drop of the lemon until the last second, and pull out just before the downturn. But since God is not one of my Facebook friends, I have to take the responsibility of finding the exit point upon myself. You will agree that finding the ultimate point is simply impossible. That is why any exit point close to the summit would be more than acceptable.

Some people might choose to exit the market when growth becomes unexplainable. This strategy makes a lot of sense on paper! The problem is that the period between that point and the ultimate summit can be incredibly long in our new reality. One, two, three, four, and sometimes even five years. So this strategy might lead you to leave a lot of money on the table. No, whether you like it or not, you don't have a choice from a specific moment to navigate in more dangerous waters where **caution will be required**. One good tip, your level of caution will have to increase proportionately as the growth of the markets becomes less and less justifiable.

In the same vein, if God sends me a text message the day before the markets starts to recover. I would go "All-In" at the very bottom, just before the very first day of recovery. But unfortunately, it doesn't work like that. While, just like on the upside, the markets will reach a certain point where the downside will no longer be justified, that's when you have to start being **bold.**

Here's the good news: "Your success as a portfolio manager does not depend on your ability to hit precisely the right exit points or the perfect entry point. In fact, if you're good (not excellent, just good), half the time, you're among the best of the best. You see, if you can take on only 50% of the market's declines while capitalizing on only 75% of the market's increases, well, congratulations, you have beaten the market by 152% since 1929.

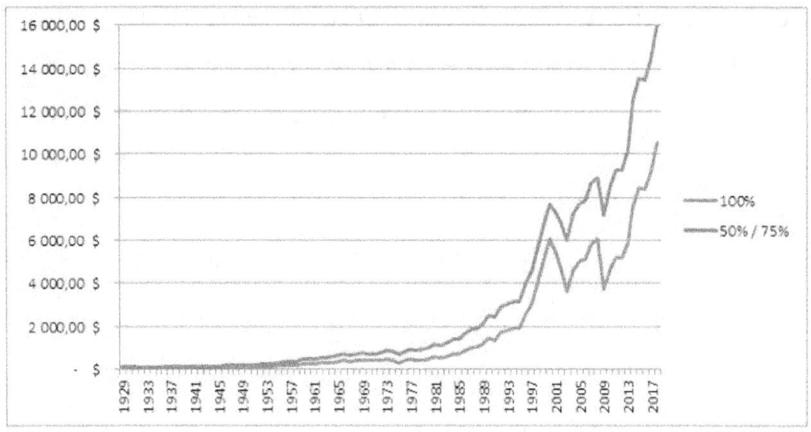

Better yet, if you have the extraordinary gift of preventing market downturns and avoiding 100% of the downturns by collecting on only 75% of the upswings, well, you just beat the S&P500 by 1435%. Even Buffett would be jealous of you.

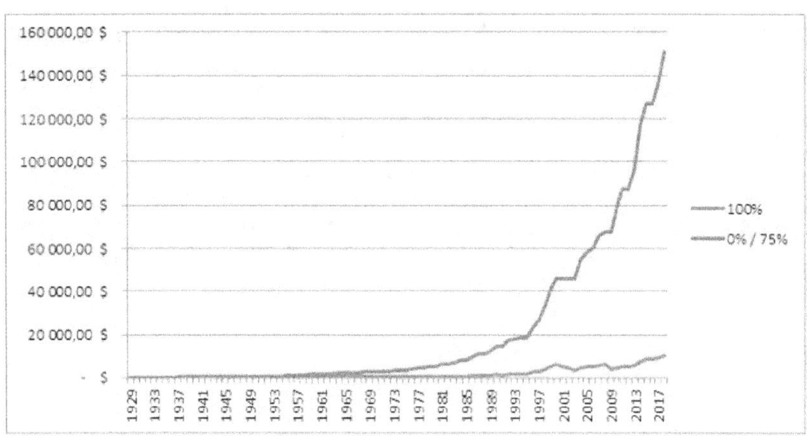

This will be my last point on the subject and, without a shadow of a doubt, the most important of the whole chapter: **Caution is**

worth much more than audacity. It is in declines that fortunes are created, not in growth.

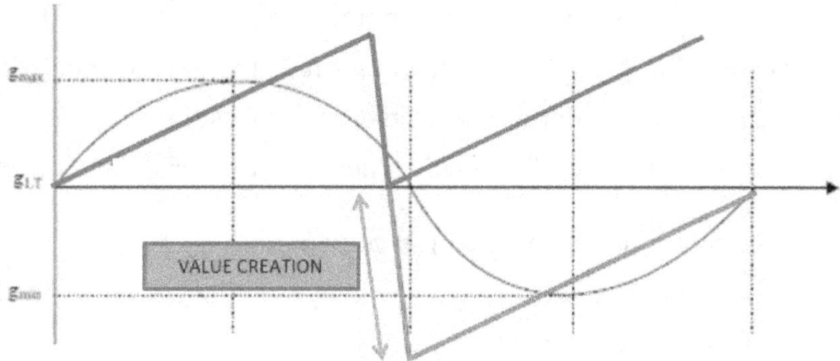

It is indeed by capturing the smallest possible drops that you will succeed in standing out. If you have $100 lose 50%, you will have to do a 100% return to return to your starting point (50$ X 50% only brings you back to 75$, right). The investor who simply lost 10% of his portfolio only needs 11% to achieve the same result.

I'll even prove it to you. Remember 2008? No. Lucky you.

I can tell you, a lot of investors remember. You see, in 2008, the market went down 50%. I told you before, the market follows a cycle, meaning that what goes down eventually goes back up. The market did come back eventually. It took 10 years, but it did. For argument's sake, you see, let's say that your portfolio went down by only 10% in 2008 (and yes, it's possible I'm living proof of it). For every 100$ bill in your portfolio in 2008, you end up with 90$ by 2009 (100$-10%). But since the market went back up 100% over the following 9 years, you would have 180$ for every bill of 100$ bill you initially had in your portfolio (90$ *+100%). Congratulation, you made +80% while the whole market made a big fat +0%. I hope you realize that the only difference between the investors who made 0% and +80% is related to a single thing. How much of the loss you did grab during the drop. I can't stress this enough: it's on the downside that you'll stand out, never on the upside.

I've always told my clients that I have two jobs.

1. To protect their capital
2. To generate a return.

In that specific order, protection first and return second. Why? Simply because protecting capital in a down market is the best way to make sure my client makes more money than everyone else at the end of the day.

I'll even push this further. If you cannot afford to have a full-time financial advisor and must choose between having one in the down market or in the upmarket. I will tell you to pick one for the down market without hesitation. That's where your financial advisor has the most added value.

I know that some of you are thinking, why not just sell everything during a down market and save both market loss and the advisor fees and to this? I respond because of the opportunity cost. If you look at the average yearly return of the S&P500 for 1999-2018, you would have made 5.92% per year. If during this period of 5000 trading days you miss out on only the 5 best days, your yearly return goes to 3.51%. Take out the top 10; you're down to 2.01%. Take out the top 20 days, and congratulation, you now have an average yearly return of -0.33%. Just to make you understand the impact on your portfolio of missing out on those top days. Let's say you have a 1,000,000$ portfolio in 1999, not missing any of those days; your portfolio would have a value in 2018 of 3,159,071$.

Otherwise, your portfolio would worth:

- -2,578,509$ (580,562$ less) if you missed the single best day
- - 1,989,788$ (1,169,283$ less) if you missed the top 5
- -1,485,947$ (1,673,124$ less) if you missed the top 10
- - 936,028$ (2,223,043$ less) if you missed the top 20

But here's the kicker, 100% of the top 5 days, top 10 days, and top 20 days happened during a market drop. The opportunity cost here could end up costing way more than your advisor fees.

"BULLS MAKE MONEY, BEARS MAKE MONEY, BUT PIGS ALWAYS GET SLAUGHTERED."

A "Bear" is an investor with a pessimistic view of the markets. A "Bull" is, in contrast, an investor with an optimistic view of the market. A "Pig" is someone greedy who has no opinion about the markets, takes excessive risk, and follows the herd. The idea behind this chapter is that no matter how positive or negative you are about the markets, it is possible either way to be successful. That said, followers who listen to analysts, take their recommendations from the newspapers, or act on the famous tips they find on the internet are inevitably heading straight for the slaughterhouse. I seem to judge the "Pigs" harshly, but I feel sorry for them because the reality is that many of these people do not deserve such a fate. And make no mistake, just because you currently have an investment advisor does not mean you are not a Pig.

How not to be a Pig? It's about getting involved in the process, it's about questioning, it's about challenging. Your manager's title is Investment <u>Advisor,</u> not Top Dog, Chief Decision Maker, or Jedi Master. His work is limited to <u>advising</u> and <u>educating</u> you. Decision-making is **your** job. I understand that you don't have the same expertise as your advisor, but that's no reason not to ask for explanations. When in doubt, remember that there are no stupid questions and no stupid answers. People tend to be impressed by the degrees, diplomas, and so-called experts.

An excellent example of this is Stanley Milgram's experiment. Stanley wanted to demonstrate how obedient people were to an authority figure. Several subjects were asked to administer an electric shock to a so-called candidate every time he failed to answer a question correctly. The teacher, of respectable age and wearing a lab coat, instructed the subject to administer the shock and to increase its power (the power ranged from mild to extreme, dangerous, and even fatal). At 75 volts, the so-called candidate grunted at each shock; at 120 volts, he complained verbally; at 150 volts, he asked to stop the experiment stipulating that he had a heart condition; at 285 volts, he screamed in agony; after which there was total silence. More than 80% of the subjects went through the 285 volts despite the cries of agony, and 62% went all the way through despite the machine clearly stating that this charge was fatal. This illustration shows you how we respond to an authority figure. Investing is about being in the business of rejection. A big part of success in investing is learning to say NO.

Don't get me wrong here; I'm not preaching against my peers or telling you that all advisors are bad. I'm just saying that since it's your money, and since you will be the one living with the consequence of your success, you should be part of the process.

Call me cynical if you want, but I personally have never listened to the analysts or recommendations of the so-called experts. Why? Because they have an agenda and their agenda is not necessarily yours. There are many examples of this. Take the example of Merrill Lynch's Henry Blodget, who during the tech bubble posted to clients, "We believe this title is proving to be a great opportunity," and simultaneously posted internally concerning the very same investment "I've never seen shit like that ."Of course, the analyst who works for a bank and covers a client company of the same bank will give you a buy recommendation on said company. I don't need to explain to you that the last thing the bank wants to do is offend its client by recommending a sale. As for the so-called experts now. Do you seriously believe that the manager of a big fund who owns 500 million shares of a company will recommend that you sell it even if he thinks it is the best thing to do? Of course not. He's going to tell you that this company is the best thing in the world since the invention of ice cream, and he's going to be the first to sell it when enough Pigs have bought it. Ask yourself this: a manager tells everyone to buy a stock that goes up 10% before it falls 30% (after the manager takes his profits, of course). His bosses will :

1. Laying him off
2. Offer him a $3 million bonus.

To ask the question is to answer it.

. . .

ANALYSTS: LAO TZU SAID, "THOSE WHO HAVE KNOWLEDGE DO not make predictions. Those who make predictions do not have knowledge". Let's assume that analysts do not have a hidden agenda for a moment. What makes you think that they simply can predict the future? You understand that their job is to guess what will happen in the future of a given company by taking for granted all the variables imaginable. What if I told you that analysts have been unable to predict the last 4 stock market crashes, that their predictions turn out to be true in only 6% of cases over a 2 year period and in only 55% of the cases over 1 year. Heads or tails here would not be far off the mark. In 2008, 91% of all stocks had a buy or better recommendation with an average expected rise in share value of 24%, while the market declined by -50%. Between 2000 and 2008, analysts could not correctly guess the market's direction (up or down) in 4 of the 9 years. Do you want to rely on this group of people for your financial decisions? It's your money, not mine. Don't get me wrong here; I sound like I'm bullying the analysts, but I don't blame them. They are asked to predict the future, nothing less... Anything else with that?

You may wonder why we still make projections if they don't even have the value of the paper they are printed on. I wonder too. The reality is that your time would be much better spent doing a detailed study of the nature, reality, challenges, and intrinsic value of the company you are interested in rather than trying to guess the future or wasting your time with those who claim to be able to.

The moral of this story: "Don't be naive ."Far be it from me to suggest that you should navigate this journey alone. My point is that you shouldn't just hand over the reins to someone else and completely detach yourself from the process.

THERE ARE ONLY TWO CERTAINTIES IN LIFE: DEATH AND TAXES

Benjamin Franklin said that there are only two certainties in life: death and taxes. Yet some people seem to have developed a compulsive obsession with trying to outsmart the tax. Personally, if I had to defy one of these two certainties, my choice would undoubtedly stop at death, but that is just me...

I understand and don't question the desire to pay as little tax as possible, but you must realize that sometimes paying tax is a good thing. In fact, one of the first things I explain to my new clients is that I am in the business of making them pay taxes, lots of taxes. Ultimately, the more taxes my clients pay, the more money I have made for them. A few years ago, I remember receiving a call from one of my good clients. The client in question was unhappy because she had just spoken to her accountant, who confirmed that she would have to pay $40,000 in taxes this year.

> - "40,000$ Franck! Do you realize my employer
>   doesn't even give me that in a year?"

> -**" You are quite right, but that's normal; we
>   made \$140,000 in profits this year."**

> -" Yes, but you don't understand, Franck: I said
>   \$40,000."

> -**" Don't worry. I have the perfect solution for
>   you! Simply return the \$140,000 in profits to
>   us, and we'll take care of your tax bill".**

> -" Well there...."

Rationality had just taken over. Unless proven otherwise, \$140,000-\$40,000 is still worth more than \$0. I concluded the conversation with my client by telling her that not only did I have no remorse for what I was making her pay in taxes, but that my goal for the following year was to make her pay even more taxes.

I'm not telling you that you should purposely pay as much tax as possible. On the contrary, I am all for minimizing tax by using every available tool at our disposal. Still, your tax bill should not be the source of financial errors at the end of the day.

Let me give you another example. Not long ago, I met with a relatively elderly prospect who asked me how I would improve his portfolio if he gave me the mandate. At first glance, a change is immediately obvious. The client in question holds 80% of his assets in a single stock. I tell the client that it would be essential to reduce the exposure to this stock to reduce the portfolio's risk. The client tells me that this is out of the question because the sale of this stock, having been purchased over 50 years ago, would generate a substantial capital gain. I politely explain to him Franklin's saying about death and taxes and that, in any case, during his lifetime or at his death, taxes will eventually become part of his reality. He doesn't want to hear it. In light of this new information, I established a new strategy for the client in which I explained that we would keep the stock in question in its integrity while hoping that the company would lose 94% of its value. At that point, we would be able to exit the position without paying taxes... Yeh!!!

The individual was so averse to paying taxes that I could never get him to understand the benefits of winding down his position so that his gains were spread over several tax years.

These are just a few examples of where our desire to reduce our taxes makes us do inappropriate things. And there are more, many more. Generating capital losses to offset capital gains can sometimes be a mistake. Return of capital investment is often a mistake. Even something as simple as contributing to your RSP can be a mistake. Don't let tax aversion influence your judgment because sometimes paying taxes is a good thing.

BUILDING A PORTFOLIO THE SAME WAY YOU WOULD BUILD A HOCKEY TEAM

You've made it this far, and I feel that for this last chapter, I should give you something of value (not that the rest was not valuable). Something that I usually don't share with everyone. My secret sauce recipe.

I still think everyone should have a financial advisor, and honestly, managing your own active portfolio is no small task. Definitely not something you can do once a week on Saturday morning in 15 minutes while sipping a cappuccino at the corner of the table. This said, I know some of you may want to do it yourselves and might even enjoy it. And I respect that. For the other ones who prefer to have a life, it's not wrong to have an idea of how it's done.

So be it. I will teach you my way. Of course, you understand that my way is not the only way, and I do not pretend that my way is the very best way. Who could pretend that? What I can tell you is that this way has proved to be very effective over the past 20 years, and check all the boxes when it comes to avoiding all the pitfalls we talked about in this book so far. But before I get into the detail of portfolio construction, I need to give you four more rules that will help you through your journey.

-RULE #1: DON'T BE OBSESSED WITH PERFECTION

The first rule when it comes to portfolio construction is not to be obsessed with reaching perfection, for there is no such thing. If anything, you don't want that. It may sound strange, but I realized over the year that most investors think that they have to pick only stuff that goes up to make money. You know why I know this? Because after 20 years at 200 review meetings per year, it seems that most clients want to focus the conversation on the investment that doesn't go as planned, or I should say, doesn't go as planned yet. It doesn't matter that the entire portfolio is making +14% and that out of 50 investments, 45 are going up. We are going to talk about the five that don't. What I'm about to tell you may sound strange. But I would not be comfortable with a portfolio where everything goes up simultaneously because this means that everything could go down at the same time as well. In reality, you can make a very decent return with a portfolio where only 50% of the asset are going up.

When you play in a poker tournament, you don't need to win every single hand to win the whole thing. In fact, you could lose most of your hands and still win the tournament, as long as you win big and lose small. An NHL hockey team does not need to win every playoff game to win the Stanley Cup. If they can manage to win more games, then they lose on every 4 out of 7 series, they will end up lifting the big trophy. You need winners and losers because market direction change constantly. You understand that no investment is an all-time winner. Today's winner will become tomorrow's loser and vice versa. That's why you don't want to have only winners in your portfolio. If you only have a winner, you will eventually only have a loser.

-RULE #2: SLOWLY BUT SURELY / STEADY GOES A LONG WAY

Now that we've established that having winners and losers is not a bad thing, we will talk about spreading the joy. Steady goes a long way when you build an investment portfolio. It's like a chess game; you need to think 3 moves in advance. Of course, your ultimate goal is that every investment you make (winners and losers) eventually generates an added value. But Franck, you just told us that having winners and losers was good. Yes, having a mix of winners and losers is good, but the idea is not to have eternal losers either. I told you before; eventually, your loser will become your winners, and they will also have their moment of glory.

I'm going back to my hockey team (sorry! I'm Canadian, and you know us Canadian and hockey, EH!). To win the game, I need to score more goals than I'm giving away (DUH!). Imagine that every player in your lineup score on average 1 goal every 5 games, and I don't know by what miracle, every single player always scores in the same game. Yes, 1 game of every 5 games will be spectacular, and yes, the team will most likely win those games (18 to something, unless, of course, you have the worst goalie in the world). But at the end of the day, the team would only win one game out of every 5 games. The team would never make the playoff and definitely never win the championship with such a result. If you want proof, check the Toronto Maple Leafs (sorry could not pass up the opportunity to take a little jab at my many colleagues from Toronto). Would the team be better if they could manage to spread their goal over the 5 games? With an average of 3.6 goals per game (18 goals / 5 games), the team would probably win 4 out 5 games and be on the very top of the league standing. The same thing goes for portfolio management. All I want is to win, and frankly, I don't care who's scoring for me today.

As long as someone does. Have you ever seen a hockey coach, after a win, tell a journalist: "yeah, that one doesn't really count because all the goals came from my fourth line players ."NO. WHO CARES? As long as someone is showing up, you're good. Steady goes a long way means that if you manage to win 4 out of 5 times, you don't need to win big. Winning my hockey game by a margin of 1 goal or by a margin of 18 goals does not change the fact that, in the end, I only have just one +1 in my win column.

I'm monitoring all my investments every day, and my target is to make a positive return of +0.1% four days out of five every week of the year. WOW, +0.1% Franck, you won't get rich fast at that paste. On the contrary. There are 250 trading days per year. If you go up 4 days out of 5, you will go up 200 days per year (250 / 5 X 4 = 200) at 0.1% per day, that's +20% per year. In fact, with the compounding effect, that's actually +28.26% per year. Remember my super formula (72 / your return = number of years required to double your portfolio). You would double your assets at that pace every 2.55 years (72 / 28.26 = 2.55 years). Steady goes a long way, which means winning small but winning often. That's all you need to do to be successful.

-RULE #3: DON'T SWING FOR THE FENCE

OK, GO, for the slow and steady approach. But How? It's elementary. Don't swing for the fence. Enough hockey, for now, let's go baseball. In baseball, your top10 Home run Hitters will hit an average of 42 home runs per year and produce 100 points but will strike out on average 170 times per year. Your best single hitters will produce 140 points and strike out 100 times per year. Swinging for the fence may sometime have a big payout but comes with more fails as well. You cannot go for those home run investments to achieve the slow and steady. Forget about those "lottery ticket investments" and focus on those sure and easy bets. I'm a real value guy. I'm buying a discounted stock that offers me a minimum of 12% but generally aims for a 24 % return. None of these 600 % potentials return speculative investment. Every year there are big winners and big losers. I made a list with the top 50 big winners and top 50 big losers of the last 10 years. It may not seem impressive if I tell you that out of those 500 big winners (50 winners X 10 years = 500), I only bought 4 (that's a batting average of 0.008). This said, out of those 500 big losers, I also only picked up 1 (damn you, Chicago Bridge and Iron (CBI)). That did not stop me from beating the market by an extensive margin (more than double, in fact) over the same period. Who needs Home run hitters when all the rest of the lineup is always getting on base?

-RULE #4: BE SMART, NOT GREEDY

Remember before when I told you to invest with a purpose? Well, as much as it's true for a single investment, it's in no way less true for your entire portfolio. I strongly believe in a goal-based approach rather than a return-based approach when it comes to investment. Making 8%, 10%, or even 20% means nothing. Reaching your life goals. That's the task at hand. Returns are only a means to an end.

Let me tell you a story. At the very beginning of my career, I was lucky enough to work in an office filled with All-Star advisors. People don't know this but making it as a financial advisor is no small task; in fact, the success rate for rookies in this business turns around 4%. So I figured, if I wanted to be part of that 4%, I might as well learn from the ones who did it before me. So I went and introduced myself to all the advisors in my office and even more from the downtown office and invited them to lunch, my treat, of course. Curious, they all wondered why the new rookie with no clients and, by the same fact, no salary would want to buy them a lunch. My answer was always the same:

"You see, I'm the kind of guy who learns from my mistake, but, in this business, I don't have the luxury of making that many mistakes. You obviously made it; otherwise, you wouldn't be sitting in that big fancy office right now. Here's the deal, I want to learn from your mistake so I can avoid them, and I want to learn your best moves so I can duplicate them. To me, this is worth at least the price of a lunch".

They all agreed, and I was able to learn so much from them. It's without any doubt the best investment I have ever made. While I was in the office of one of those advisors, I noticed that he had easily 100 picture frames on his wall. I told myself, wow, this guy is really into his family. But after further examination, I noticed that those pictures could not represent his family. It seems more like a collection of completely random people. Intrigued, I asked him about the picture frames. He replied that those were his diplomas in the most natural possible way. Your what? He then explained to me that every time he meets a new client, he asks them what the goal is. You see, people don't invest to make money; they invest to retire, travel the world, finance their kid's university, buy a 40-foot sailboat, buy a golf membership, or own an Aston Martin. Every time one of his clients reached the desired goal, the advisor would ask for a picture that he would then add to the wall. He didn't need the diplomas to give himself credibility; he had hundreds of proofs of his efficiency on the wall behind him. This guy blew my mind. This guy completely changed the way I saw this job. That's what being smart and not greedy means. Invest with a purpose.

Very often, when I make financial plan revisions with a client, I conclude that since the client is very well positioned to get all the items on their bucket list, it should reduce the risk of their overall portfolio. Almost every time, clients wonder why reduce the risk since they have had that risk level for years now and feel comfortable with it. I understand, but why take the chance. You play hockey and lead 2-0 with 2 minutes to play in the game. You don't pull your goalie to try to score a 3rd goal. That would be stupid, don't risk it if you don't need to. The same rule applies here. When it happens, I'm always giving my client 2 choices:

1. We can reduce the risk level of the portfolio.
2. He needs to find more items to add to the bucket list because we are not making money just for the sake of making money.

All this to say that, before you can start building a portfolio, you must know: 1-What you have to work with. 2-What the goal is. 3-What's the time frame, and 4-What's the level of risk you can handle. Building a portfolio without this would be like baking a cake without ingredients, a recipe, or an oven. You may, by some miracle, succeed, but most likely, it's going to be a mess.

-PORTFOLIO BUILDING 101

Once you know what you have to work with, your goal, time frame, and risk level, you will need to allocate capital to the suitable asset class based on their respective risk level, return potential, and the momentum of the actual market. Let me use another hockey analogy to show you what I mean.

A portfolio is like a hockey team, and you, as portfolio manager, are the General Manager (GM) and the Coach. As GM, your job is to ensure you have the right player on the lineup. As a Coach, your job is to know when to use which player.

Let's start with the defense. On a hockey team, the defense is supposed to protect you. It's the same thing in your portfolio. Being so, it's only fitting that all your defensive investments, take fixed income, for example, end up on your defensive lineup. On a hockey team, you don't want 6 defensemen with the same quality. You want to mix it up; you want physical guys, very defensive guys, guys with good passing skills, good hockey sense, or players with a big shot that once in a while will support the attack. The same things apply to your fixed income (defensive portfolio); you want diversity. You want short-term, long-term, floating-rate, convertible, inflation-adjusted, high yield, preferred, t-bills, and foreign bonds. The more, the merrier. What you need to know is that having all those guys on your lineup doesn't mean they always have to be on the ice. GM's job is to give his Coach options. It's the Coach's job to figure out who to use when.

The same logic applies for your offense. First, you have your wingers. Their job is plain and straightforward: attack and put the puck in the net. For your portfolio, that's your equity. I know many people don't like equity, usually because they've been burned before. You need equity; in fact, it will be your bread and butter. On top of it, a portfolio with both equity and fixed income will have a much lower risk than a portfolio filled with either one of those asset classes. I remember once, a prospect told me:

-I don't want to do equity as I am the unluckiest

*guy in the world when it comes to equity.
Every time I buy a stock, it will start falling
right away.*

-Really?

*-I swear, Franck, and on top of it, it's not like I
bought just anything here. I only bought
quality stuff that went up big over the last
year.*

Can you guess why this guy was the "unluckiest" equity investor in the world? Buy low, sell high, my friend, not the other way around. This would be like me telling you that cars are dangerous based on the fact that I had a severe car accident that nearly cost me my life a couple of years ago. But forgot to mention to you that I had 8 beers one hour before taking my car (PS: fictional, of course, I never drink). The problem here is not equity; it's the way it was used in the first place.

Years ago, I took it upon myself to build an equity portfolio that would be safe, generate significant returns and be so comfortable that even a 95-year-old client or "unluckiest" investors could own and sleep well at night. How? Using 6 simple rules that help me reduce the risk to its most basic level while not negatively affecting the returns. I told you I would share with you something I usually don't share. This is it. Here are my 6 rules to construct an equity portfolio:

-RULE #1: 15 TO 20 POSITIONS

Most finance books will tell you that to achieve maximum diversification and reduce risk to the bare minimum, you need to hold 50 stocks. What most finance books forget to tell you is that once you have 15 stocks, you have already achieved 95% diversification and that there is another way to go get that extra 5%. Following 50 companies simultaneously is a humongous task (more than a single person could handle). 15-20 is manageable.

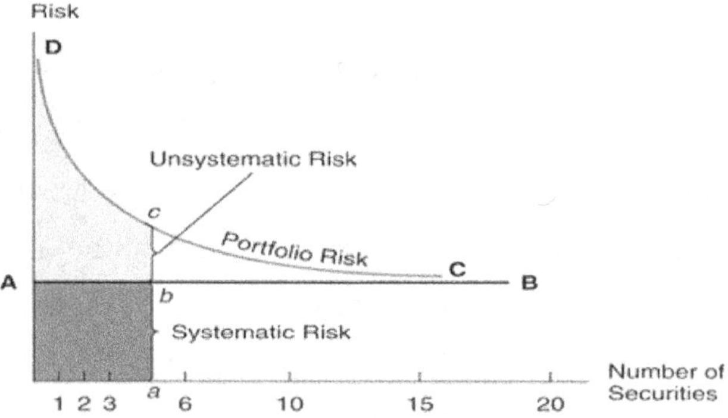

-RULE #2: 6 SECTORS AT ALL TIME

That's how we go get that extra 5% diversification. You understand that you don't have too much diversification if you buy 50 stocks, all in the energy sector. There are 10 main sectors: Healthcare, Financials, Energy, Materials, Industrials, Consumer Discretionary, Telecommunication, Consumer Staples, Utilities, and Technology. Pick at least six of them based on the state of the economy and spread your investment amongst them.

-RULE #3: CANADA AND USA SPLIT.

In Canada, the Financials, Energy, and Materials sectors account for 72% of the entire stock market (29% in the USA). In the USA. Healthcare, Consumer Discretionary, and Technology sectors account for 54% of the entire stock market (7% in Canada). Both markets are very different. Splitting your investment between both increases your diversification options.

-RULE #4: VALUE STYLE

I'm a value guy. I find bargains, purchase them and sell them once adequately priced. The value style offers way more consistency both in the short and long term, and since my six rules are all about risk reduction, it's a no-brainer.

-RULE #5: DIVIDEND COMPANY (90%)

Dividend companies offer more stability, and investors tend to be more patient with dividend-paying stocks. Historically dividend companies capture 97% of the market upswing and only 50% of the downswing. This said, I'm allowing myself to buy 1 or 2 positions that don't pay a dividend because in some sectors (i.e., technology) dividend might not be the norm.

-RULE #6: >3 BILLIONS $ COMPANY

Last but not least, I'm only buying a company with a market capitalization above 3Billions dollars. Those companies are usually more stable and provide more of the data that I need to help make my selection in the first place.

You may have noticed that I talked about my defense (fixed income) and my wingers (equity) but did not talk about my centerline. If you have ever played hockey, you know that on a line, the center's job is to support the attack by feeding the wingers, but you also support the defense by being the third defenseman on the ice. In other words, a center must sometimes be in offense and sometimes in defense. In your portfolio, that's precisely what they will do as well. They will be the investment that will allow you to actively manage your portfolio to adjust to what's happening in the market. Let me show you.

Let's say that in function of your time frame, goal, and risk aversion, you want to build a Balanced portfolio that will, at all times, have at least 40% of its asset in defense and 40% of its asset in the offense. This means that the other 20% will be your centerline. The first task will be to build your defense. Pick 5 players from your lineup that seem right for the actual market and give them ice time accordingly. Let's assume that, for the time being, interest rates are low and expected to rise and that inflation is high. I would pick short-term quality bonds and stuff that actually benefits from those conditions, like floating-rate bonds and real return investment. Then you will pick your 15-20 wingers (I know that's a lot of wingers for one hockey team) based on those 6 rules I told you about earlier. Once done, based on the state of the market, you complete your lineup with your centerline. If the market is at the beginning of the cycle and everything is rosy (the equivalent of a power play in hockey), but more offensive stuff (more stock, structured note, private investment, equity ETF…); if the market is expensive and about to correct (the equivalent of a penalty-killing in hockey) put more defensive stuff (more fixed income, money market, non-cyclical product, gold,…). Your success as a portfolio manager does not depend on your ability to predict the future but on your ability to react to what's happening. If your GM gave you all the suitable options in your lineup, the Coach should be able to make you successful no matter what the adversity is.

AFTERWORD

As all good things must come to an end, and while I could go on like this for pages and pages, I will respect my initial commitment and stop here in order not to make you nauseous. At the very beginning, I mentioned that I would give you a condensed version of the best books and articles I came across over the last 20 years, and I think I succeeded. I'm sure you will agree that although short, this book contains a ton of information. In fact, there is so much information in this book that I felt compelled to make you a summary of all the 49 tips I talked about. You will find it on the following pages. And, if you want more technical tips specifically on stock selection, go ahead and download my "Stock Picking Like a Pro 50 points Checklist" https://francknormadeau.activehosted.com/f/1

Did I succeed in making you better investors? Only you can tell me. However, one thing is certain - you are now aware

- - of our predisposition to failure
- - of the most common pitfalls you will face
- - of the danger of emotion in investing
- - of the impact of time on your wealth
- - of the notions of risk, of the benefits of active management
- - of the actual value of real estate
- - of the irrationality of the markets
- - of the mistakes that obsessing about taxes can generate and
- - of the portfolio building 101 rules

You are certainly no worse off than when you first opened this book.

I sincerely hope that you enjoyed reading my book as much as I enjoyed writing it. I invite you to rate it and leave me your comments. This is a first experience for me, and if a large majority of you inform me that I should refrain from doing this again, I swear it will be the last. But if you enjoyed the experience, let me know. You will make my day, and who knows? I might be tempted one day to release volume 2: **"Investing for not so dummy people because they have read my first book: Investing Made Simple And Easy."** OK, I agree it may be a bit long title, but I still have time to rework it.

Thank you

Franck

Leave a 1-Click Review!

Customer Reviews

★★★★★ 2
5.0 out of 5 stars ▾

5 star		100%
4 star		0%
3 star		0%
2 star		0%
1 star		0%

See all verified purchase reviews ›

Share your thoughts with other customers

Write a customer review

I would be incredibly thankful if you could take just 60 seconds to write a brief review on Amazon, even if it's just a few sentences!

>> Click here to leave a quick review

If you liked my book, I would be incredibly thankful if you could take just 60 seconds to write a brief review on Amazon, even if it's just a few sentences!

>> Click here to leave a quick review

TOP 49 TIPS SUMMARY

~

- Tip # 1 - Don't try to always be right (make a pros and cons list without the pros)
- Tip # 2 – Too much is like not enough (focus on what's really important to you)
- Tip # 3 – Sometimes it's over even if it's not (forget about the past, today, in light of what you know, would you do it)
- Tip # 4 – Don't let the story take over (if it's too good to be true, it probably is)
- Tip # 5 – Don't lose focus (take a step back to regain the big picture)
- Tip # 6 – Know when you've been lucky (have some humility)

- Tip # 7 – Don't think too highly of yourself (overconfidence costs money)
- Tip # 8 – Be patient (the stock market is a tool to transfer money from the impatient to the patient)
- Tip # 9 – Have your own independent opinion (you will never stand out by doing like everyone else)
- Tip #10 – Leave emotion behind (emotion is the cancer of your portfolio)
- Tip #11 – Buy low, sell high
- Tip #12 – Invest with a purpose (have a target and respect it)
- Tip #13 – Know when to hold them, know when to sell them (selling is the hardest thing you will have to learn to do)
- Tip #14 – Protect yourself from yourself (remove unnecessary emotion)
- Tip #15 – The past is no guarantee of the future (don't let the past influence you)
- Tip #16- Stay rational
- Tip #17- Know your shortfall. You'll be better equipped to face them
- Tip #18- The art of doing nothing (the power of compounded interest
- Tip #19- The Latte Factor (a little goes a long way)
- Tip #20- The rule of 72 (the world's fastest financial plan)
- Tip #21- Be selfish (your financial health should be in your own hands)
- Tip #22- Shop around (fees are significant)

- Tip #23- Investment advisors represent a big net added value
- Tip #24- Jumping from a plane without a parachute is no risk (Risk in uncertainty, change the way you perceive risk)
- Tip #25- You want to know how good your portfolio is (Sharpe Ratio = Return / Risk)
- Tip #26- The worst three things an advisor can do to you
- Tip #27- You must always be comfortable with your risk level no matter what
- Tip#28- Trying to be right or trying not to be wrong (be active, not passive)
- Tip #29- There is no such thing as "Too big to fail."
- Tip #30- Understand what you're buying and constantly keep your eyes on the road
- Tip #31- Real estate is not an investment
- Tip #32- Your capacity (income) is your best argument for leveraging
- Tip #33- When market nonsense actually starts making sense (understand where in the cycle we are and act accordingly)
- Tip #34- Minimize the loss to maximize the gain (protect 1st, and return will come)
- Tip #35- Always be present in the market (you cannot afford to lose the top days)
- Tip #36- Bears can win, Bulls can win, but pigs always get slaughtered (don't follow blindly, make up your own mind)

- Tip #37- Those who have knowledge do not make predictions (don't believe everything you hear or read)
- Tip #38- Don't let taxes obsession make you do stupid mistakes.
- Tip #39- Don't be obsessed with perfection when you build a portfolio (you need winners and losers)
- Tip #40- Slowly but surely, steady goes a long way (go small win most of the time)
- Tip# 41- Don't swing for the fence (go for singles and doubles; that's all you need)
- Tip #42- Be smart, not greedy (use a goal-based approach)
- Tip #43- The GM and Coach job in portfolio building
- Tip #44- Have more than 15 but less than 20 positions
- Tip #45- Have at least 6 Sectors at all time
- Tip #46- Diversify between Canada and USA
- Tip #47- Value style before growth
- Tip #48- Dividend companies are preferable
- Tip #49- At least 3 Billions $ company

Want more? I prepared an in-depth stock selection pro tips checklist with all the bells and whistles for you, my readers. Enjoy!

RESOURCES

*B.Shiv, G.Loewenstein, A.Bechara, H.Damasio and A.Damasio, "Investment Behavior and Negative Side of Emotion," Psychological Science16

*D.Kahneman "Prospect Theory (1979)

*S. Asch, "Effects of group pressure upon the modification and distortion of judgment" in Groups, Leadership, and Men (Canergie Press, 1951)

*M.Bar-Eli, O.Azar, I.Ritov, Y.Keidar-Levin, and G.Schein, "Action Bias Among Elite Soccer Goalkeepers: The Case of Penalty Kicks" (Unpublished paper, 2005)

*NYSE Factbook & Forbes (Stock market Becomes Short Attention (2018)

*L.B Alloy, L.Y. Abramson, "Judgments of contingency in depressed and non-depressed students: Sadder but Wiser?", Journal of Experimental Psychology 108 (1979): 441-485

*D.J Simons and C.F Chabris, "Gorillas in our Midst: Sustained Inattentional Blindness for Dynamic Event," Perception 28 (1999)

*Source: Thompson Reuters & Bloomberg

*G.M Cogliati, S.Paleari, S.Vismara, "IPO Pricing: Growth Rates Implied in Offer Prices" (2008)

*H. Arkes and C. Blumer, "The Psychology of Sunk Costs," Organizational Behavior and Human Decision Process 35 (1985)

*A.Dijksterhuis, M.Bos, L.Nordgren, R.Van Baaren "On making the right choice: the deliberation without attention effect" Science 311 (2007): 1005-1007

*S. Frederick, "Cognitive Reflection and Decision Making" journal of Economic Perspectives 19 (2005)

*Daily Sabah Economy "Countries-went-bankrupt in 200 years" (2015)

*Source: Canadian Real Estate Association (Statistics Canada)

*Source Andex Chart 2017

*Canadian Real Estate Association (Statistics Canada)

*T.D. Economics Special Study "Long-Term Trends in Canadian Housing Prices (2013)

*Source: Statistics Canada and Retirement Québec (Le regime en chiffre 2016)

*Source: National Association of Realtors (2006), McMansion: "A Closer Look At The Big House Trend" & L. Smith "The Truth About Real Estate Prices" (2017)

*Source: Aldridge and Krawciw (2017)